Here's all the great literature in this grade level of *Celebrate Reading!*

Flights of Fancy
Journeys of the Imagination

Featured Poet
Natalia Belting

Before Your Very Eyes

A World of Nature

Featured Poets
Marilyn Singer
Byrd Baylor
George David Weiss
Bob Thiele

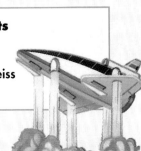

Many People, Many Voices

Stories of America

Featured Poets
Duke Redbird
Linh To Sinh My Bui

Within My Reach
The Important Things in Life

Handle with Care

Making a Difference

Featured Poets
Ouida Sebestyen
Danny Williams

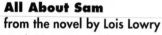

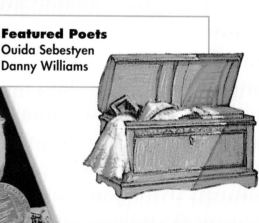

Ask Me Again Tomorrow
Growing and Changing

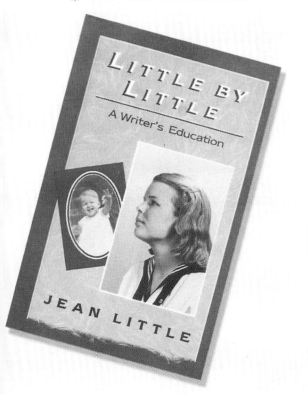

Celebrate Reading!
Trade Book Library

The Great Gerbil Roundup
by Stephen Manes

**Wayside School
Is Falling Down**
by Louis Sachar
✳ Children's Choice
✳ Parents' Choice
✳ Garden State Children's
Book Award

The Year of the Panda
by Miriam Schlein
✳ Outstanding Science Trade
Book for Children

Shiloh
by Phyllis Reynolds Naylor
✳ Newbery Medal

Taking Care of Yoki
by Barbara Campbell

A Lion to Guard Us
by Clyde Robert Bulla
✳ Notable Social Studies Trade Book

The Trading Game
by Alfred Slote
✳ Notable Social Studies Trade Book
✳ Library of Congress
Children's Book

A Taste of Blackberries
by Doris Buchanan Smith
✳ ALA Notable Children's Book
✳ Georgia Children's Book Award

The Pinballs
by Betsy Byars
✳ ALA Notable Children's Book
✳ Children's Book Award
✳ Notable Social Studies
Trade Book
✳ California Young Reader Medal
✳ Library of Congress
Children's Book

Number the Stars
by Lois Lowry
✳ Newbery Medal

The Secret Garden
by Frances Hodgson Burnett
✳ Lewis Carroll Shelf Award

The Noonday Friends
by Mary Stolz
✳ Newbery Medal Honor Book
✳ ALA Notable Children's Book
✳ Library of Congress
Children's Book

Handle With Care

MAKING A DIFFERENCE

About the Cover Artist
Douglas Faulkner is the cover photographer. The girl in the picture with the
clipboard is Barbara Bernier, a researcher who works with the manatees. The
manatee's name is "Sunrise." Mr. Faulkner lives on the Hawaiian island of Maui
and he is refurbishing a Taro Garden that belonged to a Hawaiian king.

ISBN 0-673-81161-1

1997
Scott, Foresman and Company, Glenview, Illinois
All Rights Reserved.
Printed in the United States of America.

Acknowledgments appear on page 144.

12345678910DQ010099989796

Handle With Care

MAKING A DIFFERENCE

ScottForesman

A Division of HarperCollinsPublishers

Contents

Lois Lowry Writes About Caring
Author Study

A Helping Hand

People Who Made a Difference
Genre Study

The Pet Show

BY LOIS LOWRY

Sam was at the public library with his sister and his mother late one afternoon. The public library was one of his very favorite places.

He liked to call it the *liberry,* even though everybody—his mom, his dad, his sister, and the librarian herself—had all told him about a million times that *liberry* was wrong. He knew that. He knew it was really *library.*

So he said it correctly, aloud. But to himself, Sam always said "liberry." He liked the sound of it better.

Sometimes on Saturdays, the librarian showed children's movies. *The Red Balloon* was the one that Sam liked best. It had no scary parts at all.

Winnie-the-Pooh was pretty good, too, but Sam always got a little nervous when Pooh was up in the air, dangling from the balloon, and bees came along. Sam was just a teensy-weensy bit frightened of bees.

After he had chosen his books, and the librarian had checked them out, Sam went to the bulletin board by the library's front door. He wanted to see if they would be having a movie soon. He looked all over the bulletin board for a picture of Dumbo, or Bambi, or Willy Wonka.

None of those things was there.

But Sam *did* see a sheet of pink paper with some drawings of dogs and cats. They weren't very good drawings, but you could tell they were dogs and cats.

And there were some words on the paper.

Sam screwed up his face and began to sound out the letters.

P was easy. "P, p, p," Sam sounded in a whisper.

And "T, t, t," he said.

"Pet," Sam read aloud.

Then he started on the second word. Sam knew that "Sh" was the sound of being quiet, and the second word began with "Sh."

"Pet Shhhhh," Sam said quietly. He looked at the next letter. An *O*.

"PET SHOW!" Sam yelled.

Everyone in the library turned to look at him. A man with a newspaper scowled, but most people smiled.

"That's right, Sam," the librarian said. "We're having a pet show for children on Saturday morning. With *prizes*. Do you have a pet to bring?"

Anastasia was at the counter, checking out *Gone With the Wind* for the fourteenth time. "You can't take my goldfish," she said hastily. "Frank the Second is not one bit interested in being exhibited."

"I'm afraid he doesn't have a pet," Mrs. Krupnik said to the librarian in a sad voice. "My husband is allerg——"

"I do!" Sam said. "I do! I didn't tell you! It was a secret!"

Back at home, he raced up the stairs to his room, with his mother and sister behind him. He opened his closet door, pushed aside the boots and sneakers and slippers on the floor, and found the little box he had hidden in the corner.

His mother was looking very nervous. "Sam, what do you have in there? If it's a snake or something, I really don't think I can—"

Sam took off the lid. "Shhh," he said. "He may be asleep."

"Yuck," Anastasia said, peering into the box. "It's just *dirt*."

"No, no, it's *in* the dirt! Look! I'll find him!" Carefully Sam poked through the dirt until he found his pet. "Here he is! His name is King of Worms!" Sam held the earthworm in the air.

His mother and sister stared at it. They didn't say anything.

"I could tie a ribbon around him for the pet show," Sam suggested.

"Yeah, right," said Anastasia. "Cute."

"I have to get dinner started," Mrs. Krupnik said. "Sam, be sure to wash your hands carefully after you put your, uh, your pet away. Anastasia, make sure he washes, would you?"

Anastasia nodded.

"Funny," Mrs. Krupnik murmured as she headed down the stairs. "I was going to cook spaghetti for dinner. But now I've changed my mind."

Anastasia walked with Sam to the public library on Saturday morning. Their mother and father had decided to stay at home.

"Dad would have liked to come," Anastasia told Sam, "but you know with his allergies, he was worried about being around dogs and cats."

Sam nodded. He was carrying his worm box very carefully.

"And Mom was afraid there might be rodents," Anastasia said.

"Yeah. Mom hates rodents."

They both remembered how much their mother had hated Anastasia's gerbils.

"Good thing a worm isn't a rodent," Sam said, patting his box. "Mom likes worms okay."

"And fish," Anastasia added, thinking of Frank.

They were almost at the corner, where the small brick library building was set in the middle of a big green lawn. The pet show would be on the library lawn, under the trees.

Sam could hear the sound of barking.

"A *dog* won't win first prize," he said confidently to his sister, "because dogs are ordinary."

"Let me tie your shoe tighter, Sam," Anastasia said suddenly.

She knelt on the sidewalk, and Sam looked at her in surprise. "Nobody needs to tie my shoes," he reminded her, "because Mom bought me Xerox shoes. I mean Velcro," he corrected himself.

"I really only wanted to talk to you for a minute," Anastasia explained, as she knelt beside him.

"Sam," she said, "don't be disappointed if you don't win the prize. Prizes don't matter."

"Yeah, they *do!*" Sam told her. "Prize means *best.* I think King of Worms will be the best pet! I washed him. And I changed his dirt."

"But, Sam, *every* child thinks his pet is the best. And we don't really care what the judges think, do we? As long as *we* know King of Worms is the best, that's the important thing, isn't it?"

Sam shook his head. "No," he said. "The really important thing is to win the prize."

Anastasia sighed. "Come on," she said. She stood up and took Sam's hand, the hand that wasn't holding the worm box. "Let's get it over with."

The library lawn was very noisy. Dogs were barking, babies were crying, children were shouting—Sam recognized some of his nursery school friends—and a lot of people were standing around a tree, looking up and calling to a cat, asking it please to come down.

The librarian recognized Sam and Anastasia. She gave Sam a number on a square of cardboard. "There you are," she said. "Your pet is number seventeen. And your place will be over there. Do you see the seventeen on that table? Better get in your place because the

judging will start soon. Then we'll have refreshments, afterward."

Anastasia nudged Sam over to the empty card table with the 17 taped to it. They placed the little box on the center of the table and removed the lid.

Sam poked gently in the fresh dirt until he found King of Worms. "Stick your head out," he whispered, "and look beautiful when the judges come around."

"Hey, look, Sam," Anastasia said, "somebody *did* bring a goldfish. See over there?"

They checked to make certain that Sam's worm box was safely situated on its table, and then wandered over to look at the goldfish in a bowl nearby.

"Not as good as Frank the Second," Anastasia whispered to Sam, and Sam nodded in agreement. "Not as bright-colored, not as big. And Frank's face is more intelligent."

Sam tugged suddenly on Anastasia's jeans. He pointed. "That's Nicky from my school," he whispered. "Remember Nicky the biter?"

"Well, Nicky wouldn't dare bite anyone at a pet show," Anastasia reassured Sam. They strolled over and looked into the huge box beside Nicky.

"Forty-seven gerbils," Nicky said in a loud voice.

"Nice," Anastasia said politely, and she and Sam moved away.

"And there's my friend Adam with his cat." Sam pointed. "Adam's cat is named Squeaky."

"Shhh," Anastasia said. "Look. There are the judges!"

The three men and one woman were stopping in front of the first pet, a rabbit in a cage, and discussing it. Sam could see them talking quietly to each other. One man was carrying a shopping bag. He reached into it and took out a bright blue ribbon with a badge attached to it. He wrote something on the badge and attached it to the rabbit's cage. The girl standing beside the cage grinned proudly.

"No fair!" wailed Sam. "They're giving the prize and they didn't even look at King of Worms!"

The judges had moved on to the next pet. Anastasia grabbed Sam's hand, and they ran over to the rabbit cage.

"I won!" the girl was saying happily. "My rabbit won!"

Anastasia read the words on the blue ribbon. "First Prize," she read aloud, "for Nose-wiggling."

Sam brightened. "King of Worms couldn't win that," he said, "because he doesn't have a nose."

"Look, Sam," Anastasia said. She had moved to the next pet. The judges had gone on ahead, moving from table to table, cage to cage.

"First Prize for Yellowest Pet," Anastasia read, leaning over a canary cage.

"First Prize for Largest Sleeper," she read, almost tripping over a snoring Newfoundland dog.

"First Prize for Wettest Pet," she read on the goldfish bowl.

"First Prize for Best Climber," she read on the ribbon attached to a tree trunk. From a limb above, the cat still looked down.

"First Prize for Most Pets," said the award on Nicky's huge box of gerbils.

Sam and Anastasia stood and watched quietly from a distance as the judges came to the table with the 17 on it. They saw the judges lean over the worm box.

"Maybe he'll be roundest pet," Anastasia suggested.

"I bet he'll be dirtiest," Sam said cheerfully.

They could see the judges poke gently in the dirt. One of them lifted the box. They talked some more.

"They can't decide," Anastasia whispered to Sam. "It must be a truly tough decision."

"They probably never had to do a worm before," Sam whispered back.

Finally, while they watched, the judge with the marking pen wrote on one of the blue ribbons and attached it to the worm box. Then the judges moved on.

Sam and Anastasia dashed to their table.

"Read it to me," Sam begged. "I can't read fast enough because I have to sound out all the words."

Anastasia had the ribbon in her hand and a horrified look on her face.

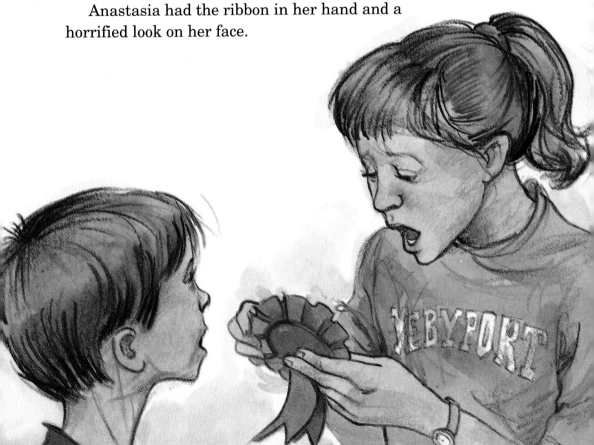

"First Prize," she read slowly, "for Most Invisible Pet."

And it was true. King of Worms was gone.

"He's bait!" Sam yowled. "I know he's bait!"

"What on earth are you talking about, Sam?" Anastasia asked. They were walking home from the pet show.

Sam couldn't stop crying. "King of Worms! I know there must have been someone there who wanted to go fishing tomorrow! And was looking for bait! And they saw King of Worms and *took* him!"

Anastasia leaned over and held a crumpled Kleenex to Sam's nose. "Here," she said. "Blow."

Sam blew his nose. "They'll put a *hook* through him," he wailed.

Anastasia shook her head. "I don't think so, Sam. I think he ran away. He just didn't want to be in a pet show."

"Worms can't run," Sam muttered. "They only crawl."

"Well, that's true. They crawl and slither. But that makes them very good at escaping."

"Why?" Sam asked.

"Because they go underground, and no one can see them. Hey, Sam, you know what? I bet King of Worms is underground right now, maybe right under our feet."

Sam sniffled, and his face brightened. "You think so? Under the sidewalk?"

"Sure," Anastasia said. "Probably slithering along down there, faster than a speeding bullet. Heading home."

Sam looked down the street, toward their house. "Probably he did want to go home, so he wouldn't have to be in a dumb pet show," he said. "Would he know the way home? Because I took him in the box, and he couldn't see anything."

"Oh, sure," his sister told him. "Worms have an excellent sense of direction. They're used to finding their way underground, where they can't see."

"Yeah," said Sam, starting to smile. "I bet he's slithering under the street right now. He doesn't even have to stop at the corner and look both ways for cars."

"He'll probably beat us home," Anastasia said.

At the corner, they stopped. Sam looked down at the drain that caught the rainwater. He knelt beside it and cupped his hands around his mouth.

"Hey, King of Worms!" he called. "I know you're down there!"

He listened for a moment. "I think I hear him," he said to Anastasia. "I hear slithering noises."

When they got to their yard, they went directly to the sandbox where Sam's big tin shovel was lying beside a dented kitchen pot.

"Where do you think he might be, Sam?" asked Anastasia.

Sam thought and then pointed. "Right here," he said. "By this bush."

Anastasia dug very carefully with Sam's shovel.

Sure enough, just a few inches below the surface, they found King of Worms.

"He beat us home," Sam said happily. "He should have won First Prize for Fastest Slitherer."

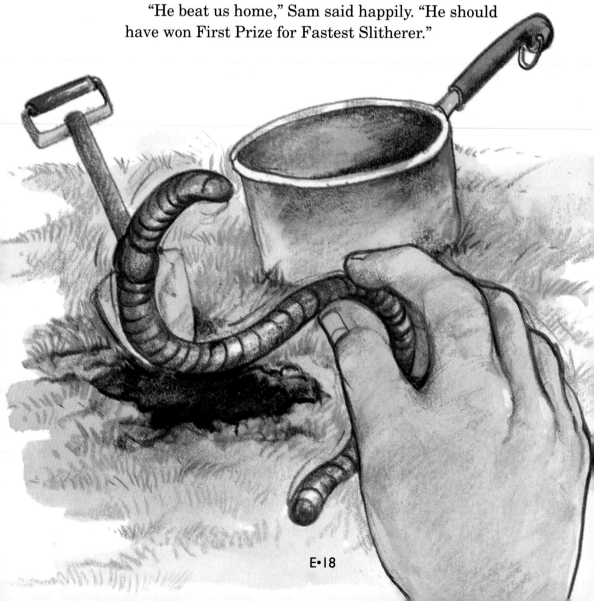

Thinking About It

1. Lost? Found? What has happened to you that helps you "connect" to the plight of Sam or Anastasia?

2. Why does Anastasia allow Sam to think that King of Worms is back home in their yard?

3. You've been asked to be the chairperson of your neighborhood's pet show. How will you publicize it? What awards will you give? What pets do you expect to see at your show?

Getting to Know Anastasia

Now that you've met Anastasia, you probably want to read one of Lois Lowry's books about her. Try one of the funniest of the Anastasia series: *Anastasia Again!*

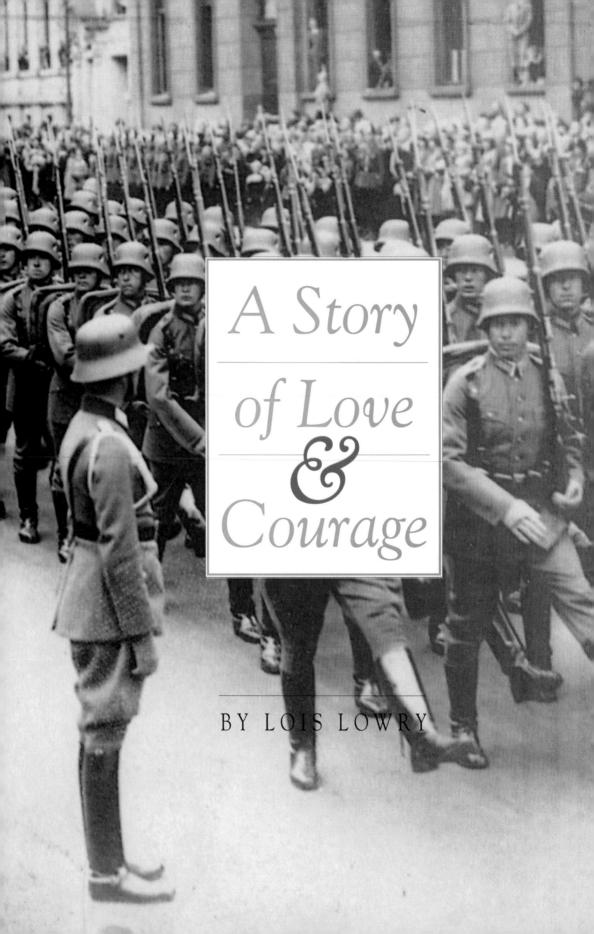

A Story
of Love
&
Courage

BY LOIS LOWRY

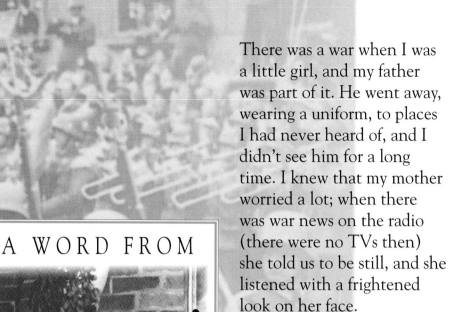

A WORD FROM

THE AUTHOR

There was a war when I was a little girl, and my father was part of it. He went away, wearing a uniform, to places I had never heard of, and I didn't see him for a long time. I knew that my mother worried a lot; when there was war news on the radio (there were no TVs then) she told us to be still, and she listened with a frightened look on her face.

Lois Lowry

It was many years later, when I was all grown up with children of my own, and even a grandchild, that I asked a friend of mine what it was like for her, when she was a child during that same war. My friend's name is Annelise—a Danish name. She grew up in Denmark, half a world away from the little Pennsylvania town where I spent my childhood.

As she began to talk, to tell me what those years were like for her, my eyes widened just as if I were a

little girl listening to an exciting story. A scary one, too. And when she had finished, my eyes were filled with tears because the story she told had such a wonderful ending. Most stories about war don't have happy endings. But this one did, so I decided that it was a story that all the children of the world should know. And I sat down to write the book that became *Number the Stars*.

Denmark is a small country in northern Europe, and it is a peaceful one. When Annelise was a little girl, it was almost a fairy tale kind of country; they had a king, and a palace, and wonderful gardens, and parks with merry-go-rounds. Many of their people were fishermen and farmers. They didn't have much of an army or a navy because they didn't think they'd ever need one. Who would want to drop bombs on a fairy tale land full of flower gardens?

Well, the Germans did. Not the Germans who invented cuckoo clocks and

Black Forest cake and lots of wonderful music; but the Germans of those years who were called Nazis and who were led by a man named Hitler. The Nazis invaded little Denmark in 1940, and the king, because he had no choice, surrendered.

Annelise told me that she woke up one morning and her country—even the quiet streets of her neighborhood—was filled with Nazi soldiers wearing helmets and carrying guns. Suddenly everything in her life changed. There was not enough food, no heat for her home in the winter. The merry-go-rounds were still. The amusement park where she had played was burned by the enemy soldiers.

Hitler had also conquered other countries in Europe. France. Holland. Norway. Belgium. And a terrible thing was happening in all of those places. The Nazis were collecting all of the Jewish people and taking them away to be killed: many, many thousands of them, even the children and babies.

Two years after Denmark surrendered to the Nazis, Annelise noticed that people she knew were disappearing: children she had played with were suddenly gone, with their families. Their houses were empty. She had never even noticed who was Jewish and who was not. But now, she realized, it was the Jewish people who were disappearing.

All of that is the scary part of the story that my friend Annelise told me. How can such a story have a happy ending?

That is what *Number the Stars* is really about: a wonderful thing that happened in a terrible time. It is about how the Christian people of Denmark decided that they would not let Hitler and the Nazis kill their Jewish friends. Without an army, without bombs or missiles, with no weapons but love and courage, they hid and saved seven thousand Jewish people.

The best thing about the story is that it really, truly happened.

Annemarie's Courage

FROM *NUMBER THE STARS*
BY LOIS LOWRY

Who Is the Man Who Rides Past?

"Tell me a story, Annemarie," begged Kirsti as she
snuggled beside her sister in the big bed they shared.
"Tell me a fairy tale."

Annemarie smiled and wrapped her arms around her
little sister in the dark. All Danish children grew up
familiar with fairy tales. Hans Christian Andersen, the
most famous of the tale tellers, had been Danish himself.

"Do you want the one about the little mermaid?"
That one had always been Annemarie's own favorite.

But Kirsti said no. "Tell one that starts with a king
and a queen. And they have a beautiful daughter."

"All right. Once upon a time there was a king,"
Annemarie began.

"And a queen," whispered Kirsti. "Don't forget
the queen."

"And a queen. They lived together in a wonderful
palace, and—"

"Was the palace named Amalienborg?" Kirsti asked
sleepily.

"Shhh. Don't keep interrupting or I'll never finish
the story. No, it wasn't Amalienborg. It was a pretend
palace."

Annemarie talked on, making up a story of a king
and queen and their beautiful daughter, Princess Kirsten;

she sprinkled her tale with formal balls, fabulous gold-trimmed gowns, and feasts of pink-frosted cupcakes, until Kirsti's deep, even breathing told her that her sister was sound asleep.

She stopped, waited for a moment, half expecting Kirsti to murmur "Then what happened?" But Kirsti was still. Annemarie's thoughts turned to the real king, Christian X, and the real palace, Amalienborg, where he lived, in the center of Copenhagen.

How the people of Denmark loved King Christian! He was not like fairy tale kings, who seemed to stand on balconies giving orders to subjects, or who sat on golden thrones demanding to be entertained and looking for suitable husbands for their daughters. King Christian was a real human being, a man with a serious, kind face. She had seen him often, when she was younger. Each morning, he had come from the palace on his horse, Jubilee, and ridden alone through the streets of Copenhagen, greeting his people. Sometimes, when Annemarie was a little girl, her older sister, Lise, had taken her to stand on the sidewalk so that she could wave to King Christian. Sometimes he had waved back to the two of them, and smiled. "Now you are special forever," Lise had told her once, "because you have been greeted by a king."

Annemarie turned her head on the pillow and stared through the partly opened curtains of the window into the dim September night. Thinking of Lise, her solemn, lovely sister, always made her sad.

So she turned her thoughts again to the king, who was still alive, as Lise was not. She remembered a story that Papa had told her, shortly after the war began, shortly after Denmark had surrendered and the soldiers had moved in overnight to take their places on the corners.

One evening, Papa had told her that earlier he was on an errand near his office, standing on the corner waiting to cross the street, when King Christian came by on his morning ride. One of the German soldiers had turned, suddenly, and asked a question of a teenage boy nearby.

"Who is that man who rides past here every morning on his horse?" the German soldier had asked.

Papa said he had smiled to himself, amused that the German soldier did not know. He listened while the boy answered.

"He is our king," the boy told the soldier. "He is the King of Denmark."

"Where is his bodyguard?" the soldier had asked.

"And do you know what the boy said?" Papa had asked Annemarie. She was sitting on his lap. She was little, then, only seven years old. She shook her head, waiting to hear the answer.

"The boy looked right at the soldier, and he said, 'All of Denmark is his bodyguard.'"

Annemarie had shivered. It sounded like a very brave answer. "Is it true, Papa?" she asked. "What the boy said?"

Papa thought for a moment. He always considered questions very carefully before he answered them. "Yes," he said at last. "It is true. Any Danish citizen would die for King Christian, to protect him."

"You too, Papa?"

"Yes."

"And Mama?"

"Mama too."

Annemarie shivered again. "Then I would too, Papa. If I had to."

They sat silently for a moment. From across the room, Mama watched them, Annemarie and Papa, and she smiled. Mama had been crocheting that evening three years ago: the lacy edging of a pillowcase, part of Lise's trousseau. Her fingers moved rapidly, turning the thin white thread into an intricate narrow border. Lise was a grownup girl of eighteen, then, about to be married to Peter Neilsen. When Lise and Peter married, Mama said, Annemarie and Kirsti would have a brother for the very first time.

"Papa," Annemarie had said, finally, into the silence, "sometimes I wonder why the king wasn't able to protect us. Why didn't he fight the Nazis so that they wouldn't come into Denmark with their guns?"

Papa sighed. "We are such a tiny country," he said. "And they are such an enormous enemy. Our king was wise. He knew how few soldiers Denmark had. He knew that many, many Danish people would die if we fought."

"In Norway they fought," Annemarie pointed out.

Papa nodded. "They fought very fiercely in Norway. They had those huge mountains for the Norwegian soldiers to hide in. Even so, Norway was crushed."

In her mind, Annemarie had pictured Norway as she remembered it from the map at school, up above Denmark. Norway was pink on the school map. She imagined the pink strip of Norway crushed by a fist.

"Are there German soldiers in Norway now, the same as here?"

"Yes," Papa said.

"In Holland, too," Mama added from across the room, "and Belgium and France."

"But not in Sweden!" Annemarie announced, proud that she knew so much about the world. Sweden was blue on the map, and she had *seen* Sweden, even though she had never been there. Standing behind Uncle Henrik's house, north of Copenhagen, she had looked across the water—the part of the North Sea that was called the Kattegat—to the land on the other side. "That is Sweden you are seeing," Uncle Henrik had told her. "You are looking across to another country."

"That's true," Papa had said. "Sweden is still free."

And now, three years later, it was *still* true. But much else had changed. King Christian was getting old, and he had been badly injured last year in a fall from his horse, faithful old Jubilee, who had carried him around Copenhagen so many mornings. For days they thought he would die, and all of Denmark had mourned.

But he hadn't. King Christian X was still alive.

It was Lise who was not. It was her tall, beautiful sister who had died in an accident two weeks before her wedding. In the blue carved trunk in the corner of this bedroom—Annemarie could see its shape even in the dark—were folded Lise's pillowcases with their crocheted edges, her wedding dress with its hand-embroidered neckline, unworn, and the yellow dress that she had worn and danced in, with its full skirt flying, at the party celebrating her engagement to Peter.

Mama and Papa never spoke of Lise. They never opened the trunk. But Annemarie did, from time to time, when she was alone in the apartment; alone, she touched Lise's things gently, remembering her quiet, soft-spoken sister who had looked forward so to marriage and children of her own.

Redheaded Peter, her sister's fiancé, had not married anyone in the years since Lise's death. He had changed a great deal. Once he had been like a fun-loving older brother to Annemarie and Kirsti, teasing and tickling, always a source of foolishness and pranks. Now he still stopped by the apartment often, and his greetings to the girls were warm and smiling, but he was usually in a hurry, talking quickly to Mama and Papa about things

Annemarie didn't understand. He no longer sang the nonsense songs that had once made Annemarie and Kirsti shriek with laughter. And he never lingered anymore.

Papa had changed, too. He seemed much older and very tired, defeated.

The whole world had changed. Only the fairy tales remained the same.

"And they lived happily ever after," Annemarie recited, whispering into the dark, completing the tale for her sister, who slept beside her, one thumb in her mouth.

Where is Mrs. Hirsch?

The days of September passed, one after the other, much the same. Annemarie and Ellen walked to school together, and home again, always now taking the longer way, avoiding the tall soldier and his partner. Kirsti dawdled just behind them or scampered ahead, never out of their sight.

The two mothers still had their "coffee" together in the afternoons. They began to knit mittens as the days grew slightly shorter and the first leaves began to fall from the trees, because another winter was coming. Everyone remembered the last one. There was no fuel now for the homes and apartments in Copenhagen, and the winter nights were terribly cold.

Like the other families in their building, the Johansens had opened the old chimney and installed a little stove to use for heat when they could find coal to burn. Mama used it too, sometimes, for cooking, because electricity was rationed now. At night they used candles for light. Sometimes Ellen's father, a teacher, complained in frustration because he couldn't see in the dim light to correct his students' papers.

"Soon we will have to add another blanket to your bed," Mama said one morning as she and Annemarie tidied the bedroom.

"Kirsti and I are lucky to have each other for warmth in the winter," Annemarie said. "Poor Ellen, to have no sisters."

"She will have to snuggle in with her mama and papa when it gets cold," Mama said, smiling.

"I remember when Kirsti slept between you and Papa. She was supposed to stay in her crib, but in the middle of the night she would climb out and get in with you," Annemarie said, smoothing the pillows on the bed. Then she hesitated and glanced at her mother, fearful that she had said the wrong thing, the thing that would bring the pained look to her mother's face. The days when little Kirsti slept in Mama and Papa's room were the days when Lise and Annemarie shared this bed.

But Mama was laughing quietly. "I remember, too," she said. "Sometimes she wet the bed in the middle of the night!"

"I did not!" Kirsti said haughtily from the bedroom doorway. "I never, *ever* did that!"

Mama, still laughing, knelt and kissed Kirsti on the cheek. "Time to leave for school, girls," she said. She began to button Kirsti's jacket. "Oh, dear," she said, suddenly. "Look. This button has broken right in half. Annemarie, take Kirsti with you, after school, to the little shop where Mrs. Hirsch sells thread and buttons. See if you can buy just one, to match the others on her jacket. I'll give you some kroner—it shouldn't cost very much."

But after school, when the girls stopped at the shop, which had been there as long as Annemarie could remember, they found it closed. There was a new padlock on the door, and a sign. But the sign was in German. They couldn't read the words.

"I wonder if Mrs. Hirsch is sick," Annemarie said as they walked away.

"I saw her Saturday," Ellen said. "She was with her husband and their son. They all looked just fine. Or at least the *parents* looked just fine—the son *always* looks like a horror." She giggled.

Annemarie made a face. The Hirsch family lived in the neighborhood, so they had seen the boy, Samuel, often. He was a tall teenager with thick glasses, stooped shoulders, and unruly hair. He rode a bicycle to school, leaning forward and squinting, wrinkling his nose to nudge his glasses into place. His bicycle had wooden wheels, now that rubber tires weren't available, and it creaked and clattered on the street.

"I think the Hirsches all went on a vacation to the seashore," Kirsti announced.

"And I suppose they took a big basket of pink-frosted cupcakes with them," Annemarie said sarcastically to her sister.

"Yes, I suppose they did," Kirsti replied.

Annemarie and Ellen exchanged looks that meant: Kirsti is so *dumb*. No one in Copenhagen had taken a vacation at the seashore since the war began. There were no pink-frosted cupcakes; there hadn't been for months.

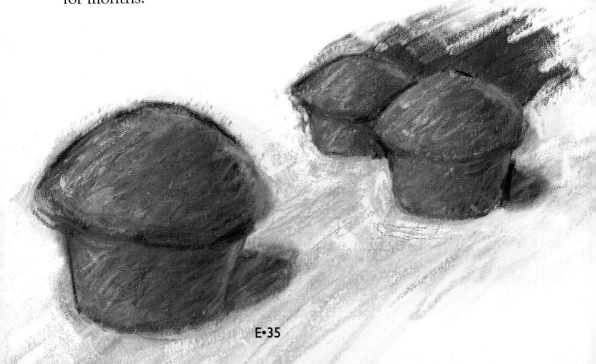

Still, Annemarie thought, looking back at the shop before they turned the corner, where was Mrs. Hirsch? The Hirsch family had gone *somewhere*. Why else would they close the shop?

Mama was troubled when she heard the news. "Are you sure?" she asked several times.

"We can find another button someplace," Annemarie reassured her. "Or we can take one from the bottom of the jacket and move it up. It won't show very much."

But it didn't seem to be the jacket that worried Mama. "Are you sure the sign was in German?" she asked. "Maybe you didn't look carefully."

"Mama, it had a swastika on it."

Her mother turned away with a distracted look. "Annemarie, watch your sister for a few moments. And begin to peel the potatoes for dinner. I'll be right back."

"Where are you going?" Annemarie asked as her mother started for the door.

"I want to talk to Mrs. Rosen."

Puzzled, Annemarie watched her mother leave the apartment. She went to the kitchen and opened the door to the cupboard where the potatoes were kept. Every night, now, it seemed, they had potatoes for dinner. And very little else.

Annemarie was almost asleep when there was a light knock on the bedroom door. Candlelight appeared as the door opened, and her mother stepped in.

"Are you asleep, Annemarie?"

"No. Why? Is something wrong?"

"Nothing's wrong. But I'd like you to get up and come out to the living room. Peter's here. Papa and I want to talk to you."

Annemarie jumped out of bed, and Kirsti grunted in her sleep. Peter! She hadn't seen him in a long time. There was something frightening about his being here at night. Copenhagen had a curfew, and no citizens were allowed out after eight o'clock. It was very dangerous, she knew, for Peter to visit at this time. But she was delighted that he was here. Though his visits were always hurried—they almost seemed secret, somehow, in a way she couldn't quite put her finger on—still, it was a treat to see Peter. It brought back memories of happier times. And her parents loved Peter, too. They said he was like a son.

Barefoot, she ran to the living room and into Peter's arms. He grinned, kissed her cheek, and ruffled her long hair.

"You've grown taller since I saw you last," he told her. "You're all legs!"

Annemarie laughed. "I won the girls' footrace last Friday at school," she told him proudly. "Where have you been? We've missed you!"

"My work takes me all over," Peter explained. "Look, I brought you something. One for Kirsti, too." He reached into his pocket and handed her two seashells.

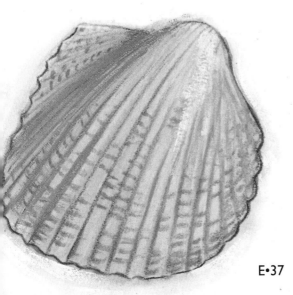

Annemarie put the smaller one on the table to save it for her sister. She held the other in her hands, turning it in the light, looking at the ridged, pearly surface. It was so like Peter, to bring just the right gift.

"For your mama and papa, I brought something more practical. Two bottles of beer!"

Mama and Papa smiled and raised their glasses. Papa took a sip and wiped the foam from his upper lip. Then his face became more serious.

"Annemarie," he said, "Peter tells us that the Germans have issued orders closing many stores run by Jews."

"Jews?" Annemarie repeated. "Is Mrs. Hirsch Jewish? Is that why the button shop is closed? Why have they done that?"

Peter leaned forward. "It is their way of tormenting. For some reason, they want to torment Jewish people. It has happened in the other countries. They have taken

their time here—have let us relax a little. But now it seems to be starting."

"But why the button shop? What harm is a button shop? Mrs. Hirsch is such a nice lady. Even Samuel—he's a dope, but he would never harm anyone. How could he—he can't even see, with his thick glasses!"

Then Annemarie thought of something else. "If they can't sell their buttons, how will they earn a living?"

"Friends will take care of them," Mama said gently. "That's what friends do."

Annemarie nodded. Mama was right, of course. Friends and neighbors would go to the home of the Hirsch family, would take them fish and potatoes and bread and herbs for making tea. Maybe Peter would even take them a beer. They would be comfortable until their shop was allowed to open again.

Then, suddenly, she sat upright, her eyes wide. "Mama!" she said. "Papa! The Rosens are Jewish, too!"

Her parents nodded, their faces serious and drawn.

"I talked to Sophy Rosen this afternoon, after you told me about the button shop," Mama said. "She knows what is happening. But she doesn't think that it will affect them."

Annemarie thought, and understood. She relaxed. "Mr. Rosen doesn't have a shop. He's a teacher. They

can't close a whole school!" She looked at Peter with the question in her eyes. "Can they?"

"I think the Rosens will be all right," he said. "But you keep an eye on your friend Ellen. And stay away from the soldiers. Your mother told me about what happened on Østerbrogade."

Annemarie shrugged. She had almost forgotten the incident. "It was nothing. They were only bored and looking for someone to talk to, I think."

She turned to her father. "Papa, do you remember what you heard the boy say to the soldier? That all of Denmark would be the king's bodyguard?"

Her father smiled. "I have never forgotten it," he said.

"Well," Annemarie said slowly, "now I think that all of Denmark must be bodyguard for the Jews, as well."

"So we shall be," Papa replied.

Peter stood. "I must go," he said. "And you, Longlegs, it is way past your bedtime now." He hugged Annemarie again.

Later, once more in her bed beside the warm cocoon of her sister, Annemarie remembered how her father had said, three years before, that he would die to protect the king. That her mother would, too. And Annemarie, seven years old, had announced proudly that she also would.

Now she was ten, with long legs and no more silly dreams of pink-frosted cupcakes. And now she—and all the Danes—were to be bodyguard for Ellen, and Ellen's parents, and all of Denmark's Jews.

Would she die to protect them? *Truly?* Annemarie was honest enough to admit, there in the darkness, to herself, that she wasn't sure.

For a moment she felt frightened. But she pulled the blanket up higher around her neck and relaxed. It was all imaginary, anyway—not real. It was only in the fairy tales that people were called upon to be so brave, to die for one another. Not in real-life Denmark. Oh, there were the soldiers; that was true. And the courageous Resistance leaders, who sometimes lost their lives; that was true, too.

But ordinary people like the Rosens and the Johansens? Annemarie admitted to herself, snuggling there in the quiet dark, that she was glad to be an ordinary person who would never be called upon for courage.

It Will Be a Long Night

Alone in the apartment while Mama was out shopping with Kirsti, Annemarie and Ellen were sprawled on the living room floor playing with paper dolls. They had cut the dolls from Mama's magazines, old ones she had saved from past years. The paper ladies had old-fashioned hair styles and clothes, and the girls had given them names from Mama's very favorite book. Mama had told Annemarie and Ellen the entire story of *Gone With the Wind*, and the girls thought it much more interesting and romantic than the king-and-queen tales that Kirsti loved.

"Come, Melanie," Annemarie said, walking her doll across the edge of the rug. "Let's dress for the ball."

"All right, Scarlett, I'm coming," Ellen replied in a sophisticated voice. She was a talented performer; she often played the leading roles in school dramatics. Games of the imagination were always fun when Ellen played.

The door opened and Kirsti stomped in, her face tear-stained and glowering. Mama followed her with an exasperated look and set a package down on the table.

"I won't!" Kirsti sputtered. "I won't ever, *ever* wear them! Not if you chain me in a prison and beat me with sticks!"

Annemarie giggled and looked questioningly at her mother. Mrs. Johansen sighed. "I bought Kirsti some new shoes," she explained. "She's outgrown her old ones."

"Goodness, Kirsti," Ellen said, "I wish my mother would get *me* some new shoes. I love new things, and it's so hard to find them in the stores."

"Not if you go to a *fish* store!" Kirsti bellowed. "But most mothers wouldn't make their daughters wear ugly *fish* shoes!"

"Kirsten," Mama said soothingly, "you know it wasn't a fish store. And we were lucky to find shoes at all."

Kirsti sniffed. "Show them," she commanded. "Show Annemarie and Ellen how ugly they are."

Mama opened the package and took out a pair of little girl's shoes. She held them up, and Kirsti looked away in disgust.

"You know there's no leather anymore," Mama explained. "But they've found a way to make shoes out of fish skin. I don't think these are too ugly."

Annemarie and Ellen looked at the fish skin shoes. Annemarie took one in her hand and examined it. It was odd-looking; the fish scales were visible. But it was a shoe, and her sister needed shoes.

"It's not so bad, Kirsti," she said, lying a little.

Ellen turned the other one over in her hand. "You know," she said, "it's only the color that's ugly."

"Green!" Kirsti wailed. "I will never, *ever* wear green shoes!"

"In our apartment," Ellen told her, "my father has a jar of black, black ink. Would you like these shoes better if they were black?"

Kirsti frowned. "Maybe I would," she said, finally.

"Well, then," Ellen told her, "tonight, if your mama doesn't mind, I'll take the shoes home and ask my father to make them black for you, with his ink."

Mama laughed. "I think that would be a fine improvement. What do you think, Kirsti?"

Kirsti pondered. "Could he make them shiny?" she asked. "I want them shiny."

Ellen nodded. "I think he could. I think they'll be quite pretty, black and shiny."

Kirsti nodded. "All right, then," she said. "But you mustn't tell anyone that they're *fish*. I don't want anyone to know." She took her new shoes, holding them disdainfully, and put them on a chair. Then she looked with interest at the paper dolls.

"Can I play, too?" Kirsti asked. "Can I have a doll?" She squatted beside Annemarie and Ellen on the floor.

Sometimes, Annemarie thought, Kirsti was such a pest, always butting in. But the apartment was small. There was no other place for Kirsti to play. And if they told her to go away, Mama would scold.

"Here," Annemarie said, and handed her sister a cut-out little girl doll. "We're playing *Gone With the Wind*. Melanie and Scarlett are going to a ball. You can be Bonnie. She's Scarlett's daughter."

Kirsti danced her doll up and down happily. "I'm going to the ball!" she announced in a high, pretend voice.

Ellen giggled. "A little girl wouldn't go to a ball. Let's make them go someplace else. Let's make them go to Tivoli!"

"Tivoli!" Annemarie began to laugh. "That's in Copenhagen! *Gone With the Wind* is in America!"

"Tivoli, Tivoli, Tivoli," little Kirsti sang, twirling her doll in a circle.

"It doesn't matter, because it's only a game anyway," Ellen pointed out. "Tivoli can be over there, by that chair. 'Come, Scarlett,'" she said, using her doll voice, "'we shall go to Tivoli to dance and watch the fireworks, and maybe there will be some handsome men there!

Bring your silly daughter Bonnie, and she can ride on the carousel.'"

Annemarie grinned and walked her Scarlett toward the chair that Ellen had designated as Tivoli. She loved Tivoli Gardens, in the heart of Copenhagen; her parents had taken her there, often, when she was a little girl. She remembered the music and the brightly colored lights, the carousel and ice cream and especially the magnificent fireworks in the evenings: the huge colored splashes and bursts of lights in the evening sky.

"I remember the fireworks best of all," she commented to Ellen.

"Me too," Kirsti said. "I remember the fireworks."

"Silly," Annemarie scoffed. "You never saw the fireworks." Tivoli Gardens was closed now. The German occupation forces had burned part of it, perhaps as a way of punishing the fun-loving Danes for their lighthearted pleasures.

Kirsti drew herself up, her small shoulders stiff. "I did too," she said belligerently. "It was my birthday. I woke up in the night and I could hear the booms. And there were lights in the sky. Mama said it was fireworks for my birthday!"

Then Annemarie remembered. Kirsti's birthday was late in August. And that night, only a month before, she, too, had been awakened and frightened by the sound of explosions. Kirsti was right—the sky in the southeast had been ablaze, and Mama had comforted her by calling it a birthday celebration. "Imagine, such fireworks for a little girl five years old!" Mama had said, sitting on their bed, holding the dark curtain aside to look through the window at the lighted sky.

The next evening's newspaper had told the sad truth. The Danes had destroyed their own naval fleet, blowing up the vessels one by one, as the Germans approached to take over the ships for their own use.

"How sad the king must be," Annemarie had heard Mama say to Papa when they read the news.

"How proud," Papa had replied.

It had made Annemarie feel sad and proud, too, to picture the tall, aging king, perhaps with tears in his blue eyes, as he looked at the remains of his small navy, which now lay submerged and broken in the harbor.

"I don't want to play anymore, Ellen," she said suddenly, and put her paper doll on the table.

"I have to go home, anyway," Ellen said. "I have to help Mama with the housecleaning. Thursday is our New Year. Did you know that?"

"Why is it yours?" asked Kirsti. "Isn't it our New Year, too?"

"No. It's the Jewish New Year. That's just for us. But if you want, Kirsti, you can come that night and watch Mama light the candles."

Annemarie and Kirsti had often been invited to watch Mrs. Rosen light the Sabbath candles on Friday evenings. She covered her head with a cloth and said a special prayer in Hebrew as she did so. Annemarie always stood very quietly, awed, to watch; even Kirsti, usually such a chatterbox, was always still at that time. They didn't understand the words or the meaning, but they could feel what a special time it was for the Rosens.

"Yes," Kirsti agreed happily. "I'll come and watch your mama light the candles, and I'll wear my new black shoes."

But this time was to be different. Leaving for school on Thursday with her sister, Annemarie saw the Rosens walking to the synagogue early in the morning, dressed in their best clothes. She waved to Ellen, who waved happily back.

"Lucky Ellen," Annemarie said to Kirsti. "She doesn't have to go to school today."

"But she probably has to sit very, very still, like we do in church," Kirsti pointed out. "*That's* no fun."

That afternoon, Mrs. Rosen knocked at their door but didn't come inside. Instead, she spoke for a long time in a hurried, tense voice to Annemarie's mother in the hall. When Mama returned, her face was worried, but her voice was cheerful.

"Girls," she said, "we have a nice surprise. Tonight Ellen will be coming to stay overnight and to be our guest for a few days! It isn't often we have a visitor."

Kirsti clapped her hands in delight.

"But, Mama," Annemarie said, in dismay, "it's their New Year. They were going to have a celebration at home! Ellen told me that her mother managed to get a chicken someplace, and she was going to roast it—their first roast chicken in a year or more!"

"Their plans have changed," Mama said briskly. "Mr. and Mrs. Rosen have been called away to visit some relatives. So Ellen will stay with us. Now, let's get busy and put clean sheets on your bed. Kirsti, you may sleep with Mama and Papa tonight, and we'll let the big girls giggle together by themselves."

Kirsti pouted, and it was clear that she was about to argue. "Mama will tell you a special story tonight," her mother said. "One just for you."

"About a king?" Kirsti asked dubiously.

"About a king, if you wish," Mama replied.

"All right, then. But there must be a queen, too," Kirsti said.

Though Mrs. Rosen had sent her chicken to the Johansens, and Mama made a lovely dinner large enough for second helpings all around, it was not an evening of laughter and talk. Ellen was silent at dinner. She looked frightened. Mama and Papa tried to speak of cheerful things, but it was clear that they were worried, and it made Annemarie worry, too. Only Kirsti was unaware of the quiet tension in the room. Swinging her feet in their newly blackened and shiny shoes, she chattered and giggled during dinner.

"Early bedtime tonight, little one," Mama announced after the dishes were washed. "We need extra time for the long story I promised, about the king and queen." She disappeared with Kirsti into the bedroom.

"What's happening?" Annemarie asked when she and Ellen were alone with Papa in the living room. "Something's wrong. What is it?"

Papa's face was troubled. "I wish that I could protect you children from this knowledge," he said quietly. "Ellen, you already know. Now we must tell Annemarie."

He turned to her and stroked her hair with his gentle hand. "This morning, at the synagogue, the rabbi told his congregation that the Nazis have taken the synagogue lists of all the Jews. Where they live, what their names are. Of course the Rosens were on that list, along with many others."

"Why? Why did they want those names?"

"They plan to arrest all the Danish Jews. They plan to take them away. And we have been told that they may come tonight."

"I don't understand! Take them where?"

Her father shook his head. "We don't know where, and we don't really know why. They call it 'relocation.' We don't even know what that means. We only know that it is wrong, and it is dangerous, and we must help."

Annemarie was stunned. She looked at Ellen and saw that her best friend was crying silently.

"Where are Ellen's parents? We must help them, too!"

"We couldn't take all three of them. If the Germans came to search our apartment, it would be clear that the Rosens were here. One person we can hide. Not three. So Peter has helped Ellen's parents to go elsewhere. We don't know where. Ellen doesn't know either. But they are safe."

Ellen sobbed aloud, and put her face in her hands. Papa put his arm around her. "They are safe, Ellen. I promise you that. You will see them again quite soon. Can you try hard to believe my promise?"

Ellen hesitated, nodded, and wiped her eyes with her hand.

"But, Papa," Annemarie said, looking around the small apartment, with its few pieces of furniture: the fat stuffed sofa, the table and chairs, the small bookcase against the wall. "You said that we would hide her. How can we do that? Where can she hide?"

Papa smiled. "That part is easy. It will be as your mama said: you two will sleep together in your bed, and you may giggle and talk and tell secrets to each other. And if anyone comes—"

Ellen interrupted him. "Who might come? Will it

be soldiers? Like the ones on the corners?" Annemarie remembered how terrified Ellen had looked the day when the soldier had questioned them on the corner.

"I really don't think anyone will. But it never hurts to be prepared. If anyone should come, even soldiers, you two will be sisters. You are together so much, it will be easy for you to pretend that you are sisters."

He rose and walked to the window. He pulled the lace curtain aside and looked down into the street. Outside, it was beginning to grow dark. Soon they would have to draw the black curtains that all Danes had on their windows; the entire city had to be completely darkened at night. In a nearby tree, a bird was singing; otherwise it was quiet. It was the last night of September.

"Go, now, and get into your nightgowns. It will be a long night."

Annemarie and Ellen got to their feet. Papa suddenly crossed the room and put his arms around them both. He kissed the top of each head: Annemarie's blond one, which reached to his shoulder, and Ellen's dark hair, the thick curls braided as always into pigtails.

"Don't be frightened," he said to them softly. "Once I had three daughters. Tonight I am proud to have three daughters again."

Who Is the Dark-Haired One?

"Do you really think anyone will come?" Ellen asked nervously, turning to Annemarie in the bedroom. "Your father doesn't think so."

"Of course not. They're always threatening stuff. They just like to scare people." Annemarie took her nightgown from a hook in the closet.

"Anyway, if they did, it would give me a chance to practice acting. I'd just pretend to be Lise. I wish I were taller, though." Ellen stood on tiptoe, trying to make herself tall. She laughed at herself, and her voice was more relaxed.

"You were great as the Dark Queen in the school play last year," Annemarie told her. "You should be an actress when you grow up."

"My father wants me to be a teacher. He wants *everyone* to be a teacher, like him. But maybe I could convince him that I should go to acting school." Ellen stood on tiptoe again, and made an imperious gesture with her arm. "I am the Dark Queen," she intoned dramatically. "I have come to command the night!"

"You should try saying, 'I am Lise Johansen!'" Annemarie said, grinning. "If you told the Nazis that you were the Dark Queen, they'd haul you off to a mental institution."

Ellen dropped her actress pose and sat down, with her legs curled under her, on the bed. "They won't really come here, do you think?" she asked again.

Annemarie shook her head. "Not in a million years." She picked up her hairbrush.

The girls found themselves whispering as they got ready for bed. There was no need, really, to whisper; they were, after all, supposed to be normal sisters, and Papa had said they could giggle and talk. The bedroom door was closed.

But the night did seem, somehow, different from a normal night. And so they whispered.

"How did your sister die, Annemarie?" Ellen asked suddenly. "I remember when it happened. And I remember the funeral—it was the only time I have ever been in a Lutheran church. But I never knew just what happened."

"I don't know *exactly*," Annemarie confessed. "She and Peter were out somewhere together, and then there was a telephone call, that there had been an accident. Mama and Papa rushed to the hospital—remember, your mother came and stayed with me and Kirsti? Kirsti was already asleep and she slept right through everything, she was so little then. But I stayed up, and I was with your mother in the living room when my parents came home in the middle of the night. And they told me Lise had died."

"I remember it was raining," Ellen said sadly. "It was still raining the next morning when Mama told me. Mama was crying, and the rain made it seem as if the whole *world* was crying."

Annemarie finished brushing her long hair and handed her hairbrush to her best friend. Ellen undid her braids, lifted her dark hair away from the thin gold chain she wore around her neck—the chain that held the Star of David—and began to brush her thick curls.

"I think it was partly because of the rain. They said she was hit by a car. I suppose the streets were slippery, and it was getting dark, and maybe the driver just couldn't see," Annemarie went on, remembering. "Papa looked so angry. He made one hand into a fist, and he kept pounding it into the other hand. I remember the noise of it: slam, slam, slam."

Together they got into the wide bed and pulled up the covers. Annemarie blew out the candle and drew the dark curtains aside so that the open window near the bed let in some air. "See that blue trunk in the corner?" she said, pointing through the darkness. "Lots of Lise's things are in there. Even her wedding dress. Mama and Papa have never looked at those things, not since the day they packed them away."

Ellen sighed. "She would have looked so beautiful in her wedding dress. She had such a pretty smile. I used to pretend that she was *my* sister, too."

"She would have liked that," Annemarie told her. "She loved you."

"That's the worst thing in the world," Ellen whispered. "To be dead so young. I wouldn't want the Germans to take my family away—to make us live some-place else. But still, it wouldn't be as bad as being dead."

Annemarie leaned over and hugged her. "They won't take you away," she said. "Not your parents, either. Papa promised that they were safe, and he always keeps his promises. And you are quite safe, here with us."

For a while they continued to murmur in the dark, but the murmurs were interrupted by yawns. Then

Ellen's voice stopped, she turned over, and in a minute her breathing was quiet and slow.

Annemarie stared at the window where the sky was outlined and a tree branch moved slightly in the breeze. Everything seemed very familiar, very comforting. Dangers were no more than odd imaginings, like ghost stories that children made up to frighten one another: things that couldn't possibly happen. Annemarie felt completely safe here in her own home, with her parents in the next room and her best friend asleep beside her. She yawned contentedly and closed her eyes.

It was hours later, but still dark, when she was awakened abruptly by the pounding on the apartment door.

Annemarie eased the bedroom door open quietly, only a crack, and peeked out. Behind her, Ellen was sitting up, her eyes wide.

She could see Mama and Papa in their nightclothes, moving about. Mama held a lighted candle, but as Annemarie watched, she went to a lamp and switched it on. It was so long a time since they had dared to use the strictly rationed electricity after dark that the light in the room seemed startling to Annemarie, watching through the slightly opened bedroom door. She saw her mother look automatically to the blackout curtains, making certain that they were tightly drawn.

Papa opened the front door to the soldiers.

"This is the Johansen apartment?" A deep voice asked the question loudly, in the terribly accented Danish.

"Our name is on the door, and I see you have a flashlight," Papa answered. "What do you want? Is something wrong?"

"I understand you are a friend of your neighbors the Rosens, Mrs. Johansen," the soldier said angrily.

"Sophy Rosen is my friend, that is true," Mama said quietly. "Please, could you speak more softly? My children are asleep."

"Then you will be so kind as to tell me where the Rosens are." He made no effort to lower his voice.

"I assume they are at home, sleeping. It is four in the morning, after all," Mama said.

Annemarie heard the soldier stalk across the living room toward the kitchen. From her hiding place in the narrow sliver of open doorway, she could see the heavy uniformed man, a holstered pistol at his waist, in the entrance to the kitchen, peering in toward the sink.

Another German voice said, "The Rosens' apartment is empty. We are wondering if they might be visiting their good friends the Johansens."

"Well," said Papa, moving slightly so that he was standing in front of Annemarie's bedroom door, and she could see nothing except the dark blur of his back, "as you see, you are mistaken. There is no one here but my family."

"You will not object if we look around." The voice was harsh, and it was not a question.

"It seems we have no choice," Papa replied.

"Please don't wake my children," Mama requested again. "There is no need to frighten little ones."

The heavy, booted feet moved across the floor again and into the other bedroom. A closet door opened and closed with a bang.

Annemarie eased her bedroom door closed silently. She stumbled through the darkness to the bed.

"Ellen," she whispered urgently, "take your necklace off!"

Ellen's hands flew to her neck. Desperately she began trying to unhook the tiny clasp. Outside the bedroom door, the harsh voices and heavy footsteps continued.

"I can't get it open!" Ellen said frantically. "I never take it off—I can't even remember how to open it!"

Annemarie heard a voice just outside the door. "What is here?"

"Shhh," her mother replied. "My daughters' bedroom. They are sound asleep."

"Hold still," Annemarie commanded. "This will hurt." She grabbed the little gold chain, yanked with all her strength, and broke it. As the door opened and light flooded into the bedroom, she crumpled it into her hand and closed her fingers tightly.

Terrified, both girls looked up at the three Nazi officers who entered the room.

One of the men aimed a flashlight around the bedroom. He went to the closet and looked inside. Then with a sweep of his gloved hand he pushed to the floor several coats and a bathrobe that hung from pegs on the wall.

There was nothing else in the room except a chest of drawers, the blue decorated trunk in the corner, and a heap of Kirsti's dolls piled in a small rocking chair. The flashlight beam touched each thing in turn. Angrily the officer turned toward the bed.

"Get up!" he ordered. "Come out here!"

Trembling, the two girls rose from the bed and followed him, brushing past the two remaining officers in the doorway, to the living room.

Annemarie looked around. These three uniformed men were different from the ones on the street corners.

The street soldiers were often young, sometimes ill at ease, and Annemarie remembered how the Giraffe had, for a moment, let his harsh pose slip and had smiled at Kirsti.

But these men were older and their faces were set with anger.

Her parents were standing beside each other, their faces tense, but Kirsti was nowhere in sight. Thank goodness that Kirsti slept through almost everything. If they had wakened her, she would be wailing—or worse, she would be angry, and her fists would fly.

"Your names?" the officer barked.

"Annemarie Johansen. And this is my sister—"

"Quiet! Let her speak for herself. Your name?" He was glaring at Ellen.

Ellen swallowed. "Lise," she said, and cleared her throat. "Lise Johansen."

The officer stared at them grimly.

"Now," Mama said in a strong voice, "you have seen that we are not hiding anything. May my children go back to bed?"

The officer ignored her. Suddenly he grabbed a handful of Ellen's hair. Ellen winced.

He laughed scornfully. "You have a blond child sleeping in the other room. And you have this blond daughter—" He gestured toward Annemarie with his head. "Where did you get the dark-haired one?" He twisted the lock of Ellen's hair. "From a different father? From the milkman?"

Papa stepped forward. "Don't speak to my wife in such a way. Let go of my daughter or I will report you for such treatment."

"Or maybe you got her someplace else?" the officer continued with a sneer. "From the Rosens?"

For a moment no one spoke. Then Annemarie, watching in panic, saw her father move swiftly to the small bookcase and take out a book. She saw that he was holding the family photograph album. Very quickly he searched through its pages, found what he was looking for, and tore out three pictures from three separate pages.

He handed them to the German officer, who released Ellen's hair.

"You will see each of my daughters, each with her name written on the photograph," Papa said.

Annemarie knew instantly which photographs he had chosen. The album had many snapshots—all the poorly focused pictures of school events and birthday parties. But it also contained a portrait, taken by a photographer, of each girl as a tiny infant. Mama had written, in her delicate handwriting, the name of each baby daughter across the bottom of those photographs.

She realized too, with an icy feeling, why Papa had torn them from the book. At the bottom of each page, below the photograph itself, was written the date.

And the real Lise Johansen had been born twenty-one years earlier.

"Kirsten Elisabeth," the officer read, looking at Kirsti's baby picture. He let the photograph fall to the floor.

"Annemarie," he read next, glanced at her, and dropped the second photograph.

"Lise Margrete," he read finally, and stared at Ellen for a long, unwavering moment. In her mind, Annemarie pictured the photograph that he held: the baby, wide-eyed, propped against a pillow, her tiny hand holding a silver teething ring, her bare feet visible below the hem of an embroidered dress.

The wispy curls. Dark.

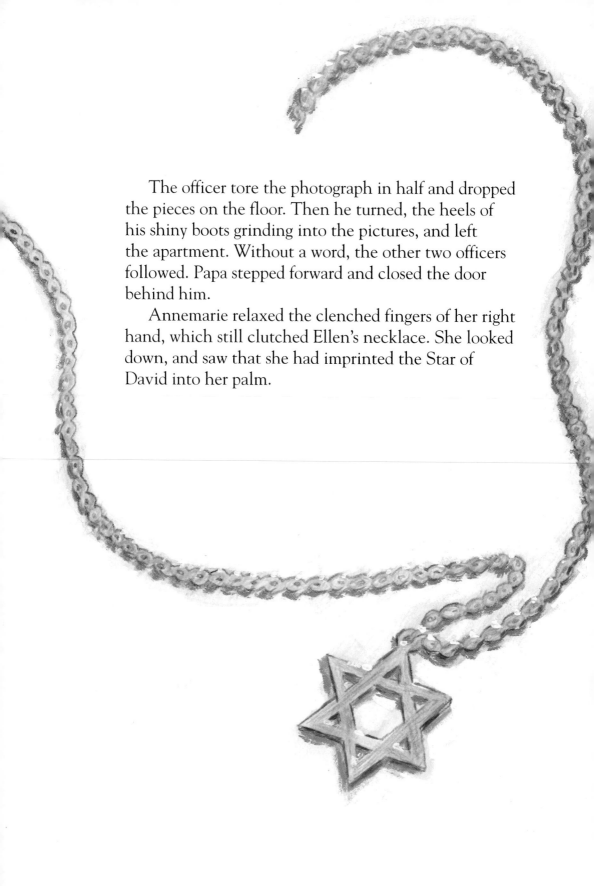

The officer tore the photograph in half and dropped the pieces on the floor. Then he turned, the heels of his shiny boots grinding into the pictures, and left the apartment. Without a word, the other two officers followed. Papa stepped forward and closed the door behind him.

Annemarie relaxed the clenched fingers of her right hand, which still clutched Ellen's necklace. She looked down, and saw that she had imprinted the Star of David into her palm.

Thinking
About It

1. If you had been in the bedroom with Annemarie and Ellen when the Nazi officer was questioning them, what would you have done? Would you have said anything, or would you have simply watched?

2. The author finishes the selection by telling us that Annemarie had the Star of David imprinted in her hand. Why not just leave off with a description of the Nazi officers' exit from the house?

3. How would you make sure that everyone who reads this selection remembers the brave moment in Annemarie's life?

by Ann M. Martin

What's the Sign for

Jessi?

Two things have helped Jessi Ramsey make the adjustment to a new town: ballet lessons and a new friend, Mallory Pike, who got Jessi into the Baby-sitters Club. Now Jessi has taken on the club's most challenging assignment—baby-sitting for a deaf child. Before she begins, Jessi must learn more about Ameslan (am'ə slan), one kind of sign language.

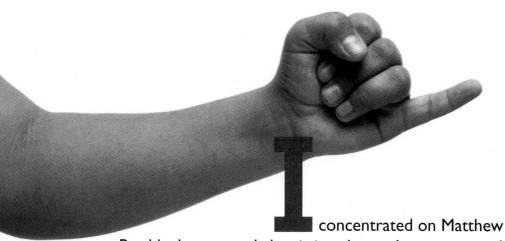

I concentrated on Matthew Braddock, my new baby-sitting charge. I was supposed to go to his house for my first training session. I decided that before I did, I should at least know what Ameslan was. So the night before I met Matthew I went into our den and looked up some things in our encyclopedia. It turns out Ameslan is sign language and that signing is a way of talking with your hands—so that deaf people can see you talk, since they can't hear you. The book says signing is a lot easier than reading lips, because so many spoken words "look" the same. Stand in front of a mirror. Say "pad" and "bad." Do they look any different? Or try "dime" and "time." Do *they* look any different? Not a bit.

But signing is a language especially designed for the deaf, in which words or concepts are represented by different signs made with the hands. Actually, there are different kinds of sign languages, just like there are different spoken languages. American Sign Language (or Ameslan) was the language Matt had learned.

When I thought about it, even people who can hear use signs pretty often. We have always accused Daddy of "talking with his hands." He absolutely cannot hold them still when he talks. If he's talking about something big, he holds his hands wide apart. If he's trying to make a point, he pounds one hand on the table. If he wants to show that something is unimportant, he sort of waves one hand away. If he says your name, he points to you at the same time.

Well, I couldn't imagine a different sign for every word in the world, and I couldn't imagine the sign for a word like "shoe." Or how, for instance, would the sign for apple be different from the sign for orange?

I would find out soon enough.

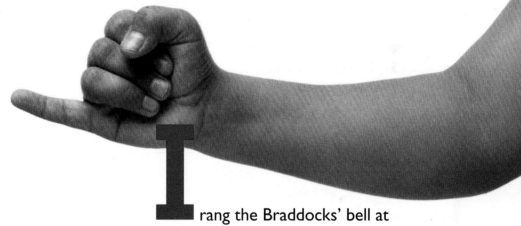

I rang the Braddocks' bell at 3:15 on a Monday afternoon. I realized that from then on, my schedule was going to be very busy. Mondays— Braddocks, then a meeting of the Baby-sitters Club. Tuesdays—dance class. Wednesdays—same as Mondays. Thursdays—only free afternoon. Fridays—dance class, then club meeting.

Whew!

The door was answered by a pixie of a girl who must have been Haley, but who looked small for nine. Her blonde hair was cut short with a little tail in the back (*very in*), and her brown eyes were framed by luscious dark lashes. Her face was heart-shaped, and she gave me this wide, charming grin that showed a dimple at the right corner of her mouth.

"Hi," she said. "Are you Jessica?"

"Yup," I replied, "but call me Jessi. You must be Haley."

"Yup." (That grin again.) "Come on in."

Haley opened the door and I walked into a house that looked pretty much like Mallory's, only without all the kids. A lot of the houses in this neighborhood look the same. They were all built by this one guy, Mr. Geiger. I guess he didn't have much imagination.

As soon as I stepped inside, I was greeted by Mrs. Braddock. She looked like a nice, comfortable kind of mom to have. She was wearing blue jeans and Reeboks and a big, baggy sweater, and she rested one hand reassuringly on Haley's shoulder while shaking my hand with the other.

"Hi, Jessica—" she began.

"Jessi, Mommy," Haley interrupted. "Call her Jessi."

Mrs. Braddock and I laughed, and I was ushered into the living room. Then Mrs. Braddock told me to sit on the couch. "Matt hasn't come home from school yet, but he'll be here any minute. As you know, I'm not going out this afternoon. I mean, you're not here for official baby-sitting. I just want you to meet Matt and Haley, and I want to introduce you to sign language. If you're interested in learning it, we'll go on from there."

"Okay," I said. "Let's start. I love languages."

Mrs. Braddock smiled. "Terrific."

"Can I be the teacher, Mommy?" asked Haley.

"Does Haley know sign language, too?" I asked.

"We all do," replied Mrs. Braddock. "It's the only way to communicate with Matt, and we don't want him left out of anything." She turned to Haley. "You better be the assistant teacher, honey," she told her. "Why don't you start by finding the *American Sign Language Dictionary?* We'll lend it to Jessi for awhile."

Haley ran off and Mrs. Braddock continued. "Before I begin showing you actual signs, I should tell you a little about teaching the deaf, I guess. One thing you ought to know is that not everyone agrees that the deaf should communicate with sign language. Some people think they should be taught to speak and to read lips. However, in lots of cases, speaking is out of the question. Matt, for instance, is what we call profoundly deaf. That means he has almost total hearing loss. And he was born that way. We're not sure he's ever heard a sound in his life. He doesn't even wear hearing aids. They wouldn't do him any good. And since Matt can't hear any sounds, he can't hear spoken words, of course, and he can't imitate them either. So there's almost no hope for speech from Matt. Nothing that most people could understand anyway."

"And lip reading is hard," I said. "I experimented in front of the mirror last night."

"You've been doing your homework," said Mrs. Braddock approvingly.

"How come everyone wants deaf people to speak and read lips?" I asked.

"Because if they could, they'd be able to communicate with so many more *hearing* people. Matt, for instance, can only communicate with us and with the teachers and students at his school. None of our friends knows sign language and only a few of our relatives do. When Matt grows older, he'll meet other deaf people who use sign language, and maybe even a few hearing people who can sign, but he'll be pretty limited. Imagine going to a movie theater and signing that you want two tickets. No one would know what you meant."

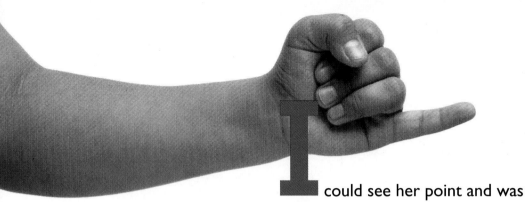

I could see her point and was about to ask why the Braddocks had chosen signing for Matt, when Mrs. Braddock continued. "We're not sure we've made the right choice, but that's the choice we made. At least we've been able to communicate with Matt for a long time now. Most kids take years to learn lip reading and feel frustrated constantly, even at home." Mrs. Braddock sighed. "Some families," she added, "don't bother to learn to sign. The deaf children in those families must feel so lost."

Haley returned with a big book then and dropped it in my lap. "Here's the dictionary," she said cheerfully.

I opened it to the middle and looked at the pages in front of me. I was in the K section. The book reminded me of a picture dictionary that Becca used to have.

"Key" was the sixth word under K. I saw a picture of two hands—one held up, the other imitating turning a key in an imaginary lock on the upright hand.

"Oh, I get it!" I said. "This looks like fun."

"It is sort of fun," agreed Mrs. Braddock. "But there are several thousand signs in there."

"Several *thousand!*" I cried. I knew there were a lot of words in the world, but I hadn't thought there were *that* many.

"Don't worry," said Mrs. Braddock. She took the dictionary from me and closed it. "Right now, I'm just going to teach you a few of the signs that Matt uses the most. When you're at home you can use the dictionary to look up other things or things you forget, okay?"

"Okay," I replied, feeling relieved.

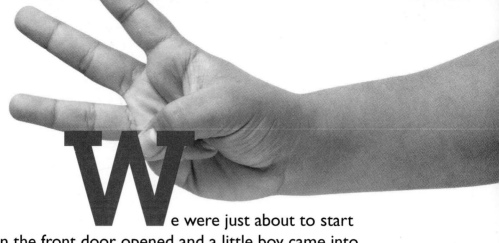

We were just about to start when the front door opened and a little boy came into the living room. I caught sight of a van backing down the Braddocks' driveway.

"Well, there you are!" cried Mrs. Braddock, speaking with her voice and her hands at the same time. "Home from school."

The boy was Matt, of course, and his face broke into a grin just like Haley's, with a dimple on the right side of his mouth. He waved to his mother and then ran to her for a hug.

"Believe it or not," Mrs. Braddock said to me, "that wave was the sign for 'hello.' It's also the sign for 'good-bye.' "

"That's easy to remember," I said.

Mrs. Braddock turned Matt so that he could look at me. Then she turned him back to her and once again began signing and talking at the same time. She was introducing us.

"Is there a sign for my *name?*" I asked, amazed.

"That's a good question," Mrs. Braddock replied. "And the answer is 'Not exactly,' or perhaps, 'Not yet.' What I did just now was spell your name. I used finger spelling, which I'll explain later. However, since it takes too long to spell out names we use a lot, such as our own names, or the names of Matt's teacher and his friends at school, we make up signs for those people." Mrs. Braddock signed something to Matt, saying at the same time, "Matt, show Jessi the sign for your name."

Matt grinned. Then he held up one hand and sort of flew it through the air.

"That," said Mrs. Braddock, "is the letter M for Matt being tossed like a baseball. Matt loves sports."

"Oh!" I exclaimed. "Neat."

"Show Jessi the sign for Haley," Mrs. Braddock instructed Matt.

Another hand flew through the air.

"That was the letter H soaring like Halley's Comet.

When you know finger spelling, you'll be able to tell the signs apart more easily. Also, we'll have to give you a sign soon."

Mrs. Braddock asked Haley to take Matt into the kitchen then and fix him a snack. When we were alone again, she began showing me signs.

"The word 'you' is easy," she told me. "Just point to the person you're talking to."

(What do you know? I thought. My father knows sign language!)

"To sign 'want,' " Mrs. Braddock went on, "hold your hands out like this—palms up, fingers relaxed—and pull them toward you, curling your fingers in slightly."

Mrs. Braddock went on and on. She showed me signs for foods, for parts of the body, and for the words "bathroom," "play," and "come." Finally she said, "I think that's enough for one day. I'm going to start dinner. Why don't you take Matt and Haley downstairs to the rec room so you can get to know them better?"

The Braddocks' rec room looked like any other rec room—a TV, a couple of couches, a shelf full of books, and plenty of toys.

"Ask Matt what he wants to play," I said to Haley.

Haley obediently signed to her brother, a questioning look on her face. Matt signed back.

"He wants to read," Haley told me.

"Read!" I cried. "He can read?"

"Well, he *is* seven," Haley pointed out, "and he's been in school since he was two. It's really important for him to be able to read and write."

Of course, I thought. Reading and writing are other ways to communicate.

Matt found a picture book and curled up with it.

"How can I get to know him if he reads?" I wondered out loud.

"How about getting to know *me*?" asked Haley impatiently, and she shot a brief look of annoyance at her brother. Luckily he didn't notice.

That one annoyed look said a lot. Something was going on between Matt and Haley, I thought, but I wasn't sure what.

That night I finished my homework and settled into bed with the *American Sign Language Dictionary*. Tons of questions came to me, and I wrote them down so that I'd remember to ask Mrs. Braddock. How do you sign a question? Do you make a question mark with your fingers? How do you make a word plural?

I mean, if there's a sign for "apple," what's the sign for "apples"? What's finger spelling? (Mrs. Braddock had forgotten to explain.) And can you string signs into sentences, just like when you're speaking? (I wasn't sure, because I couldn't find signs for "the," or "an," or "a.") Even though I knew I had a lot to learn, I decided I liked sign language. It's very expressive—almost like dancing.

Wednesday

Brat, brat, brat.
Okay. We all agree that Jenny is spoiled and a little bratty, but I've never minded her too much. At least not until today. Today she was at her worst. Mostly, she just didn't want to do anything. She wasn't dressed for anything fun and she wouldn't change into play clothes. Finally, I took her outside and we ran into Jessi and the Braddocks! Then Jenny's brattiness just came pouring out. That kid needs a few lessons in manners. Really. Maybe we should start a class.[1]

---

[1] an entry in the Baby-sitters Club notebook

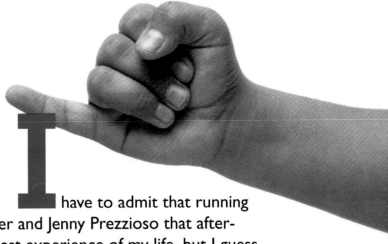

I have to admit that running into Mary Anne Spier and Jenny Prezzioso that afternoon was not the best experience of my life, but I guess it could have been worse. And it absolutely was not Mary Anne's fault. I bet Jenny was born a brat.

Oh, well. I'm ahead of myself (again). Mary Anne's afternoon at the Prezziosos' house began right after school ended. Mrs. P. let Mary Anne inside, where she found Jenny sitting at the dining room table having a snack. Now, come on. How many kids do *you* know who get afternoon snacks in the dining room? At our house, it's strictly kitchen. Usually we don't even sit down. Becca and I just open the fridge, stand in front of it until we see something we want, take it out, and eat it on the way to our rooms or (in my case) on the way to a baby-sitting job or to Stamford for dance class.

But Jenny was sitting at the dining room table eating pudding from a goblet with a silver spoon. She was wearing one of her famous lacy dresses. (Mary Anne once told me that she thinks the Prezziosos support the U.S. lace industry all by themselves.) On her feet were white patent leather Mary Janes, and in her hair were silky blue ribbons.

Now don't get me wrong. Jenny wasn't off to a birthday party or anything. Her mother dresses her like that every day. (I hope the time will come when Jenny will rebel and refuse to wear lace anymore. Or ruffles. Or ribbons. Or bows.) Another thing. The Prezziosos are not rich. They're just average. But Jenny is their princess, their only child. (They call her their angel.)

Anyway, Mrs. Prezzioso finally left, and Mary Anne and Jenny were on their own.

"Finish up your pudding, Jen, and then we can play some games," said Mary Anne brightly.

"I eat slowly," Jenny informed her. "And don't call me Jen."

(Keep in mind that Jenny is only four.)

"Sorry," Mary Anne apologized. But already her hackles were up, because she added tightly, "I didn't mean to insult you."

Jenny slurped away at her pudding. "All finished," she announced a minute later, holding out the spoon and goblet.

"Great," replied Mary Anne. "Go put them in the sink." She wasn't going to do Jenny's work for her.

Jenny did so, scowling all the way.

Mary Anne knew they were off to a bad start and began to feel guilty. "Okay!" she said. "Let's play a game. How about Candy Land? Or Chutes and Ladders?"

Jenny put her hands on her hips. "I don't wanna."

"Then let's read. Where's *Squirrel Nutkin*? That's your favorite."

"No, it isn't, and I don't *wanna* read."

Jenny and Mary Anne were facing off in the kitchen, Jenny's hands on her hips.

"I know!" cried Mary Anne. "Finger painting!"

"Finger painting?" Jenny sounded awed. "Really?"

"Yes. . . . If you'll change into play clothes."

"No. No no no. This is my new dress and I'm wearing it."

"Okay, fine," replied Mary Anne. "If there's nothing you want to do then you can just stand here all afternoon. I'm going to read a book." (As you can probably imagine, quiet Mary Anne doesn't say things like that very often.)

Jenny looked at Mary Anne with wide eyes. "You mean you're not going to play with me?"

Mary Anne sighed. "What do you want to play?" she asked.

"I don't know."

"Dolls?"

"Nope."

"House?"

"Nope."

"You want to draw a nice picture for your mommy?"

"Nope."

Mary Anne had reached the end of her rope. "That does it," she muttered. She opened a closet door, pulled out Jenny's light coat (of course Jenny didn't own a sweat shirt or a windbreaker or anything), and put it on her. She buttoned it up, Jenny protesting the whole time, put on her own jacket, and marched Jenny outdoors.

"Now," said Mary Anne grimly, "we're going to have fun if it kills us."

But Jenny, if you remember, was wearing white patent leather shoes. They're kind of hard to have fun in. The only activity Mary Anne could think of for them was a nice quiet walk.

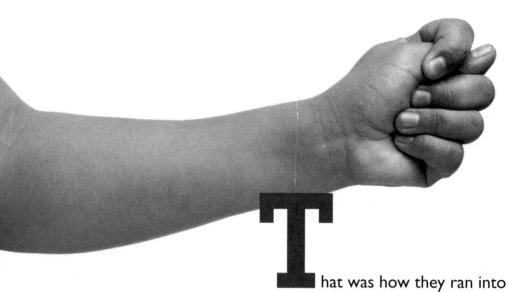

That was how they ran into Matt and Haley and me. I was at the Braddocks again and had just had another signing lesson. I had memorized over twenty signs by then. (The Braddocks knew about a million, but I was new at this. They'd been at it for years.) Anyway, after the lesson, Mrs. Braddock had asked me to take Matt and Haley outside to play.

Mary Anne and I were surprised to see each other.

"Hi!" we exclaimed.

Then we had to do a lot of introducing, since Jenny didn't know me or the Braddocks, Mary Anne didn't know the Braddocks, I didn't know Jenny, and the Braddocks didn't know Jenny or Mary Anne.

Haley translated for Matt, and I jumped in whenever I knew a sign. I noticed that Jenny was watching us with her mouth open.

"What are you doing?" she finally asked Haley and me.

"Matt's deaf," I explained. "He can't hear us, but we can tell him things with our hands. Then he can see what we're saying."

Jenny approached Matt and yelled right into his ear at the top of her lungs, "CAN'T YOU HEAR ME?"

Matt just blinked and backed up a few paces.

Haley signed to him to say hi to Jenny.

Matt obediently waved.

"He just said hi to you," I told Jenny.

"You mean he can't talk, either?" asked Jenny, aghast.

"He can make *sounds*," Haley told her defensively.

And just then, Matt caught sight of a bug wriggling along the sidewalk. He laughed. His laugh was a cross between fingernails on a blackboard and a goose honking. I had to admit, it was one weird sound.

Jenny cringed against Mary Anne. "Let's go," she whispered—loudly enough for Haley and me to hear her. "He's weird. I don't want to play with him."

"Well, you're not the first one to say so!" Haley shouted.

"We better leave," Mary Anne said quickly. "I'm sorry, Jessi. I'll call you tonight so we can talk, okay?"

I nodded.

As they left, Haley shot a murderous glance at her brother, who was now on his hands and knees, watching the bug.

"You know what?" she said to me, and her great grin was gone. "Having a brother like Matt really stinks." Then she stood behind him, tears glistening in her eyes, and shouted, "You stink, Matt! You STINK!" Of course, Matt didn't hear her.

"It is so horrible!" Haley went on. "People think Matt's weird, but he isn't. Deaf is not weird. Everybody's unfair." Then she stormed into the Braddocks' house and slammed the door behind her.

Ah-ha, I thought. I was beginning to understand Haley and Matt. The Braddocks had just moved to a new neighborhood and Haley wanted to fit in, but Matt was making that a little difficult.

Well, I could sympathize. In Stoneybrook, being black wasn't any easier.

My first real baby-sitting job for Haley and Matt! I have to tell you that I was a little nervous. I was even more nervous than I'd felt at the most recent rehearsal of *Coppélia*.[2] The rehearsal had been hard work and I'd felt sore afterward, but not nervous. I was fairly self-confident. So if I could dance the lead in a ballet, you'd think that a job baby-sitting for a nine-year-old and a seven-year-old one afternoon wouldn't be hard at all. And ordinarily it wouldn't be. But Matt is not your ordinary seven-year-old.

I still knew only a handful of signs, so I started imagining all sorts of problems. What if Haley wasn't around and Matt didn't feel well? I couldn't ask him what was wrong, and if he tried to tell me, I probably wouldn't understand.

But there was no point in worrying about things like that. Of course Haley would be there to help me, and Matt would be fine. Besides, he could write, and anyway, Mrs. Braddock was only going to the grocery store. She'd be gone for an hour and a half, tops.

When I got to the Braddocks' house I could tell that Mrs. Braddock was a little nervous, too. She kept reminding me about things.

"Be extra careful outdoors," she said. "Remember that Matt can't hear car horns."

"Right," I replied.

[2] a ballet in which Jessi is dancing

"And he can't hear a shouted warning."

"Right."

"And inside he can't hear the doorbell or telephone."

"I'll take care of those things."

"Do you remember the sign for 'bathroom'?"

"Yup."

"For 'eat'?"

"Yup. . . . And I can do finger spelling. I memorized the alphabet last night." (Mrs. Braddock had explained to me that there was a sign for every letter in the alphabet, just like there were signs for words. So, for instance, if I wanted to spell my name, I would sign the letters J-E-S-S-I. Finger spelling takes longer than regular signing, but at least you can communicate names and unusual words that way.) "The whole alphabet?" Mrs. Braddock repeated. She sounded impressed.

I nodded. "The whole thing. Oh, and I thought of a name for myself. Look."

I shaped my right hand into the sign for the letter J (for my name), pointed it downward, and whisked it back and forth across the palm of my left hand. That's the sign for the word "dance" except that you usually make a V with your right index and middle fingers, to look like a pair of legs flying across the floor.

"See?" I said. "A dancing J! Anyway, don't worry, Mrs. Braddock. You know how many signs I've memorized. I'm not too good at sentences, but Matt and I will get along. No problem." I sounded a lot more confident than I felt.

"Besides," added Haley, who had appeared in the kitchen. "You've got *me*, right?" She sounded a little uncertain—as if I might say I didn't need her after all.

I put my arm around Haley. "I'll say!" I exclaimed. "You're the best help I've got."

Haley turned on that smile of hers.

"Well . . ." said Mrs. Braddock. She glanced down the hallway and out the front door, looking (I think) for Matt's special school bus. "Matt should be here in about ten minutes. I told him this morning that you would be here when he got home from school and that I'd be back soon. Haley can help you remind him if he seems anxious, but I think he'll be all right. He really likes you, Jessi."

"Thanks," I replied.

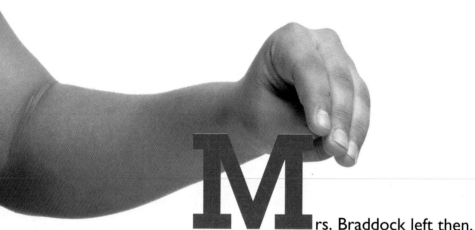

Mrs. Braddock left then, and Haley and I sat on the front stoop to wait for Matt. The school bus was prompt. It pulled into the driveway exactly ten minutes after Mrs. Braddock left.

Matt jumped down the steps of the van. He waved eagerly to the driver, who waved back, and then signed something to a giggling face that was pressed against a window of the van. The little boy signed back. A second boy joined in. Matt and his friends were talking about football. (I think.)

It was odd, I thought, to see so much energy and so much communication—without any sound at all. Watching the boys was like watching TV with the volume turned off.

The bus drove away and Matt ran across the lawn to Haley and me, smiling. (Mrs. Braddock hadn't needed to worry about anxiety.)

"Hi!" I signed to Matt. (A wave and a smile.)

He returned the wave and smile.

I showed him the sign for my name (which he liked), and then I asked him about school. (The sign for school is clapping hands—like a teacher trying to get the attention of her pupils. When I found that out, I wondered what the sign for "applause" or "clap" is, since it seemed to have been used up. This is the sign: You touch your hand to your mouth, which is part of the sign for "good," and *then* clap your hands. It's like applauding for good words. See why I like languages? They make so much sense.)

Matt signed back, "Great!" (He pointed to his chest with his thumb and wiggled his fingers back and forth—with a broad grin.)

After Matt had put his schoolbooks in his room, he ate a quick snack. I'll give you the sign for the snack. See if you can guess what the snack was. You form your hand into the sign for the letter A, then you pretend to eat your thumb. That's the sign for . . . apple! Eating the letter A. Isn't that great?

Anyway, as soon as Matt was finished eating, I took him and Haley outdoors. I had a plan. I hadn't been able to stop thinking about what happened when the Braddocks and I ran into Mary Anne and Jenny Prezzioso. And I was determined that Matt and Haley were going to make friends in their new neighborhood. I remembered how horrible Becca had felt when nobody in Stoneybrook would play with her. Then one day Charlotte Johanssen, who's just her age, had come over, and Becca was so happy she barely knew what to do.

I began marching Matt and Haley over to the Pikes' house.

"Where are we going?" Haley asked me.

"We," I replied, "are going to a house nearby where you will find eight kids."

"Is one of them my age?" Haley sounded both interested and skeptical.

"Yup," I replied and suddenly realized that we were leaving Matt out of the conversation by not signing. I told Haley to sign.

"I hope the nine-year-old isn't a boy," Haley said, hands flying.

(Matt made a face at that.)

"Nope," I said. "The nine-year-old is a girl. Her name is Vanessa. She likes to make up rhymes." There was no way I could sign all that, so Haley did it for me, to keep Matt informed. Then she told him where we were going.

"Is there a seven-year-old Pike?" Matt signed.

Haley looked at me.

I nodded. Then I signed "girl," and Matt made a horrible face. It wasn't a sign, but it could only mean one thing—YUCK!

"Tell him there's an eight-year-old boy," I said to Haley.

Matt brightened, and I finger spelled N-I-C-K-Y.

We had reached the Pikes' front door by then. Matt boldly rang the bell. It was answered by Mallory, and I was relieved. I'd told her we might come over, and I wanted her to help me with the introductions.

"The Barretts are here, too," she whispered, as we stepped inside. "They're friends from down the street. Buddy is eight and Suzi is five." She turned to Haley and Matt, said hello, and waved at the same time. She knew that much about signing from me. I loved her for remembering to do it. That's one of the reasons she's my new best friend.

"Well," said Mallory, "everyone's playing in the backyard."

We walked through the Pikes' house, waving to Mrs. Pike on the way, and stepped into the yard. It looked like a school playground.

The Pikes and the Barretts all stopped what they were doing and ran to us.

The introductions began.

The signing began.

The explaining began.

The staring began.

And Haley began to look angry again.

I glanced at Mallory. "Ick-en-spick," she whispered. And with that, a wonderful idea came to me. Mallory and I love to read, and not long ago we'd both read a really terrific book (even if it was a little old-fashioned) called *The Secret Language,* by Ursula Nordstrom. These two friends make up a secret language, and "ick-en-spick" is a word they use when something is silly or unnecessary.

"You know," I said to the kids, "maybe Matt can't hear or talk, but he knows a *secret language.* He can talk with his *hands.* He can say anything he wants and never make a sound."

"Really?" asked Margo (who's seven) in a hushed voice.

Mallory smiled at me knowingly. "Think how useful that would be," she said to her brothers and sisters, "if, like, Mom and Dad punished you and said, 'No talking for half an hour.' You could talk and they'd never know it."

"Yeah," said Nicky slowly. "Awesome."

"How do you do it?" asked Vanessa. "What's the secret language?"

This time, Haley jumped in with the answer. "It's this," she replied. She began demonstrating signs. The kids were fascinated.

"Say something," Claire, the youngest Pike, commanded Matt.

"He can't hear you," I reminded Claire.

"*I'll* tell him what you said," Haley told Claire importantly. She signed to Matt.

Matt began waving his hands around so fast that all I could understand was that he was signing about football again.

Haley translated. "Matt says he thinks the Patriots are going to win the Super Bowl this year. He says—"

"No way!" spoke up Buddy Barrett. Haley didn't have to translate that. Matt could tell what Buddy meant by the way he was shaking his head.

Matt began signing furiously again.

"What's he saying? What's he saying?" the kids wanted to know.

Mallory and I grinned at each other. We sat down on the low wall by the Pikes' patio, relieved, and watched the kids.

"Your brothers and sisters are great," I said.

"When you grow up in a family as big as mine," Mallory replied, "you end up being pretty accepting."

"Thank goodness."

After a while I looked at my watch and realized that Mrs. Braddock would probably be back from the grocery store soon.

"I better take Haley and Matt home," I said and began to round them up. But in the end, I only brought Matt home. Haley was having too much fun at the Pikes' to leave, and swore up and down that she knew the way back to her house. I left her teaching the kids how to sign the word "stupid." I had a feeling there was going to be a lot of silent name-calling in the neighborhood for a while.

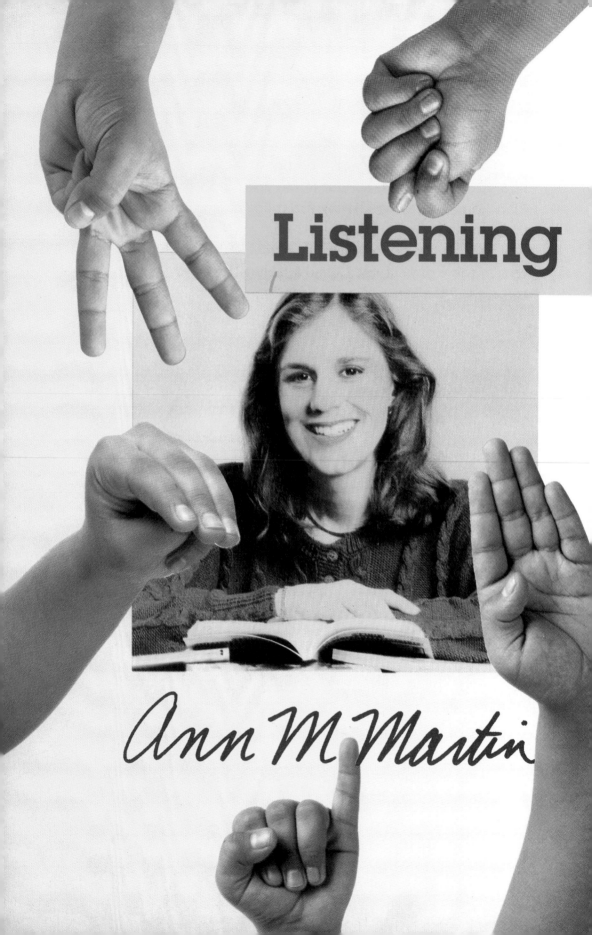

To Each Other

by Ann M. Martin

Once I saw two people communicating—using sign language. They were signing very fast, using not only their hands but their bodies and faces. I thought signing was beautiful, like dancing.

Later, I saw a play called *Children of a Lesser God,* and then I saw the movie as well. Many of the characters in this story are hearing impaired and communicate with sign language. After I saw the movie, I decided to learn more about signing— especially after I realized that some of my readers are hearing impaired.

In *Jessi's Secret Language,* Matt, who is profoundly deaf, finds himself in a difficult situation. At first, Matt can't communicate with the hear- ing children in his new neigh- borhood because they can't sign. Then Jessi becomes his baby-sitter and begins to learn some sign language. She teaches some sign language to other members of the Baby-sitters Club. They teach it to their charges as a special new activity. Soon children all over Stoneybrook are using this exciting "secret language," and Matt is able

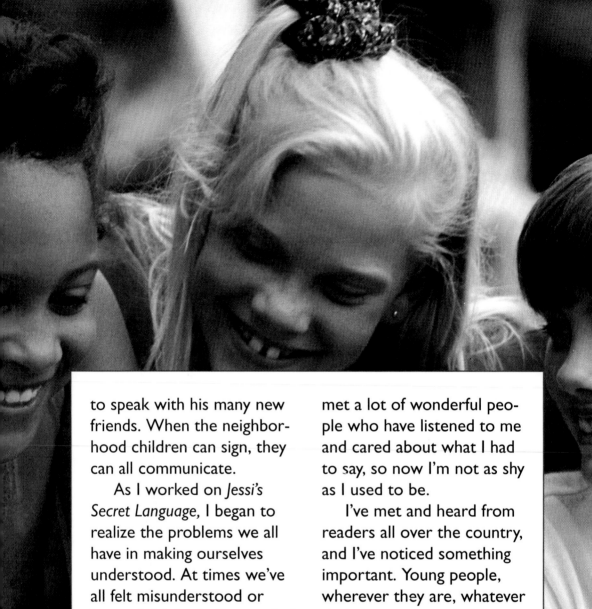

to speak with his many new friends. When the neighborhood children can sign, they can all communicate.

As I worked on *Jessi's Secret Language,* I began to realize the problems we all have in making ourselves understood. At times we've all felt misunderstood or ignored. Nobody likes to feel that he or she is not being listened to. When I was younger, I had a hard time getting people to listen to me because I was so shy. It was difficult for me to speak to other people without feeling nervous. As I've gotten older, though, I've met a lot of wonderful people who have listened to me and cared about what I had to say, so now I'm not as shy as I used to be.

I've met and heard from readers all over the country, and I've noticed something important. Young people, wherever they are, whatever their interests or their strengths or weaknesses, want to be listened to and understood. They want to know that they have friends and family who care about what they think.

And you know what? It's just the same for grown-ups!

Thinking About It

1. Many people who read about the Baby-sitters Club feel that they almost know the characters. How well do you know Jessi? How well can you see and hear her? What's she like?

2. Matt's family had to make a decision. They had to choose between sign language and lip reading as a way for Matt to communicate. Did they make the right choice for Matt? Why or why not?

3. Jessi realizes she has to learn some sign language in order to care for Matt. She creates a dancing *J* to represent herself. What symbol or sign would you create for yourself?

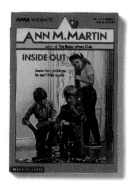

More...and...More... and More!

If you haven't already read some of the other Baby-sitters Club books, you're probably on your way to the library now to check one out. While you're there, take a look at *Inside Out.* It's a book by Ann M. Martin about a boy named Jonno and his autistic brother, James.

The Pigeons at Embarcadero Center

by Danny Williams, age 9
Illustration by Jennifer Phelan, age 10

I like the ones with white wings
with black stripes
some look like ducks
some look like chickens
some look like rich people in new clothes
there's one now
cleaning his wing
with his beak
they are scared of people
kids try to catch them
some peck at the feet of old guys
sitting on benches
the old guys look like they think
the pigeons might ask them
for money
some pigeons are ruffled
like they've been around a long time
some of the people digging in
garbage cans for food
look like they've been around
with the pigeons
they feed the food they find
to the pigeons
they too are scared of people
they walk away
their black plastic bags empty
flapping in the wind
like wings

A Niche in the Kitchen

BY OUIDA SEBESTYEN

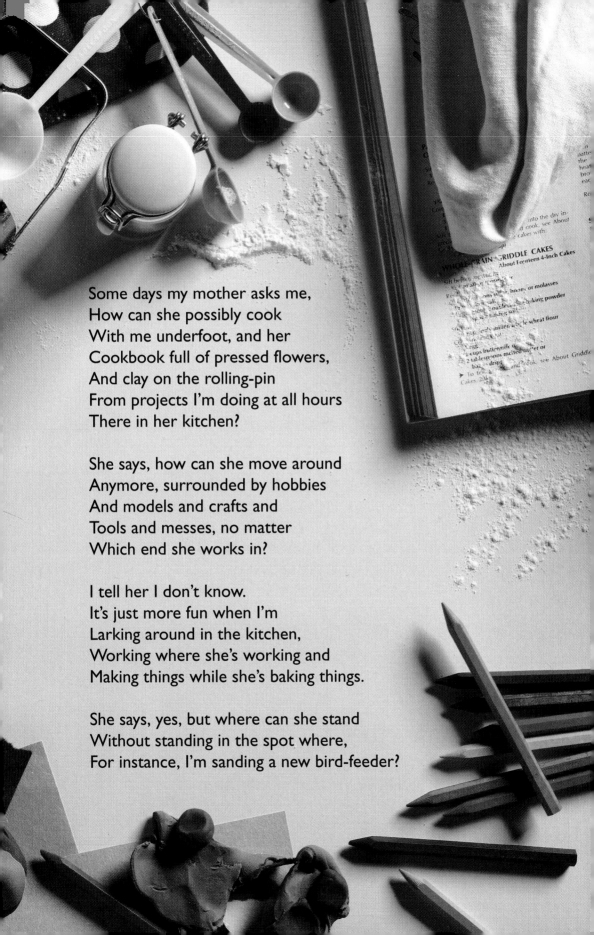

Some days my mother asks me,
How can she possibly cook
With me underfoot, and her
Cookbook full of pressed flowers,
And clay on the rolling-pin
From projects I'm doing at all hours
There in her kitchen?

She says, how can she move around
Anymore, surrounded by hobbies
And models and crafts and
Tools and messes, no matter
Which end she works in?

I tell her I don't know.
It's just more fun when I'm
Larking around in the kitchen,
Working where she's working and
Making things while she's baking things.

She says, yes, but where can she stand
Without standing in the spot where,
For instance, I'm sanding a new bird-feeder?

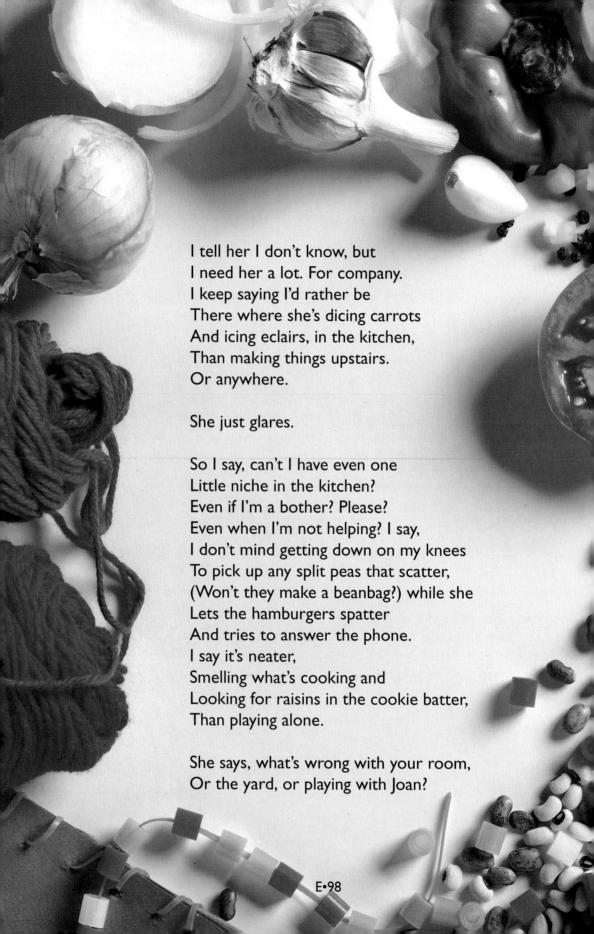

I tell her I don't know, but
I need her a lot. For company.
I keep saying I'd rather be
There where she's dicing carrots
And icing eclairs, in the kitchen,
Than making things upstairs.
Or anywhere.

She just glares.

So I say, can't I have even one
Little niche in the kitchen?
Even if I'm a bother? Please?
Even when I'm not helping? I say,
I don't mind getting down on my knees
To pick up any split peas that scatter,
(Won't they make a beanbag?) while she
Lets the hamburgers spatter
And tries to answer the phone.
I say it's neater,
Smelling what's cooking and
Looking for raisins in the cookie batter,
Than playing alone.

She says, what's wrong with your room,
Or the yard, or playing with Joan?

I explain to her, well, it's just nicer
Knowing she's right on my heels
Behind me, slicing bologna
Or spicing the applesauce.
But she's the boss,
And if that's how she feels
I'd better just gather my stuff up
And go.

She says, well . . . no.

I say, no?

She says, no, that time will come soon enough.
Too soon. So just bring your stuff
Back into the kitchen.

She smiles and gives me a taste of
Tomato paste and makes more room
On the counter beside her, so I can lace
The pieces of wallet from my leather kit
Or do some tooling.
Working together like that for a bit
Is great. I string beads
While she strings beans,
Or I glue seeds to plaques,
Or illustrate books between
Racks of cake-layers cooling.

My mother says, when she was young
A kitchen was where everyone hung around
Telling what happened that day
And feeling at home.
She says it had a table for schoolwork
And mending and crewel, and
A stool for cutting hair,
And not so much chrome.
She liked it there.

I say I like it here, too, in this kitchen,
And I'm glad it's okay if I stay.
We get on with whatever we're making —
Shaking the steak in flour and
Squashing papier-mâché in a tray —
Feeling like artists
And getting in each other's way.
She doesn't scream
When she opens the oven and
Steam pours out of the mouth
Of the voodoo mask I'm baking.
She only sighs when the poster I'm drying
Falls into the bacon she's frying.

Every once in a while
She tells me it probably would be grand
To have a kitchen no bigger than a minute —
So small that only one person could fit in it.
But then she folds a slice of warm bread
And puts my favorite jam between,
And I know she doesn't mean it.

I know when she laughs and
Gives my hair a muss,
And swipes the counter to clear a spot,
She's saying our kitchen will always be
Large enough for both of us —
For her, and the things she likes a lot,
And the things I like a lot,
And me.

GARRETT A. MORGAN

By Glennette Tilley Turner

Everyone who has ever crossed a street safely with the help of a traffic light can thank Garrett A. Morgan. He is the inventor who thought of a way for people and cars to take turns crossing at intersections.

Garrett A. Morgan was born in Paris, Tennessee, on March 4, 1875. His parents, Sydney and Elizabeth Reed Morgan, had ten other children. Times were hard and at age fourteen Morgan struck out on his own—heading for nearby Cincinnati, Ohio. He found a job as a handyman.

Four years later he moved to Cleveland, Ohio. He arrived with only a quarter to his name, but he had a talent for fixing mechanical things—and for saving his money. He got a job as a sewing machine adjuster at the Roots and McBride Company. Before long he had thought of an idea. It was a belt fastener for sewing machines.

Garrett Morgan soon saved enough money to buy his own sewing machine business and purchase a home. His father had died by that time and he invited his mother to move to Cleveland. A year later he married Mary Anne Hassek. They enjoyed a long, happy marriage and were the parents of three sons.

Morgan was a good businessman. Before long he was able to open a tailoring shop in which he hired thirty-two employees. His shop made suits, dresses, and coats with sewing equipment he had built.

Although planning was important to his success, his next business venture came about by accident. He was trying to find a liquid chemical that he could use to polish sewing machines. While he was experimenting, his wife called him to dinner. Hurriedly, he wiped his hands on a pony-fur cloth on his workbench and the wiry fur hairs straightened out. Curious to see how this liquid would affect other kinds of hair, he tried it out on the Airedale dog next door. The dog's hair got so straight that his owner hardly recognized him. After a bit more experimenting, Morgan put the chemical on the market as a product to straighten hair.

His next invention was a safety hood or "breathing device." In more recent years it has been called a gas mask. Morgan received a patent for it (U.S. Patent No. 1,113,675) and as he stated: "The object of the invention is to provide a portable attachment which will enable a fireman to enter a house filled with thick suffocating gases and smoke and to breathe freely for some time therein, and thereby enable him to perform his duties of saving life and valuables without danger to himself from suffocation."

The safety hood won a first prize gold medal from the International Exposition for Sanitation and Safety. The judges at the exposition immediately recognized its value. Morgan wanted to market his invention, but he believed prejudice would limit his sales if his racial identity was generally known. He knew that some fire departments would rather endanger their firemen's lives than do business with a black inventor. He attempted to solve this problem in a most unusual way. He formed the National Safety Device Company. He was the only nonwhite officer. The other officers—one of whom had been the director of public works for the city of Cleveland—would arrange for demonstrations of the device and set up a canvas tent in the demonstration area. They would set a fire in the tent with an awful-smelling fuel made of tar, sulphur, formaldehyde, and manure. Once the fire was roaring, Morgan would appear disguised as an Indian chief. He'd put on the gas mask and go in and remain up to twenty minutes while he extinguished the flames.

He would come out as good as new. This might have gone on indefinitely, but the night of July 25, 1916, changed everything. Morgan became a hero overnight.

That night there was a violent explosion at the Cleveland Waterworks. Approximately thirty workmen were trapped in a tunnel five miles out and more than 225 feet beneath Lake Erie. Smoke, natural gases, and debris kept would-be rescuers from entering the tunnel where the workmen were trapped. Family and friends didn't know whether anyone had survived the blast.

Finally, someone at the site of this disaster remembered that Garrett Morgan had invented a gas mask. It was about two o'clock in the morning when Morgan was called in. He, his brother Frank, and two volunteers put on gas masks and entered the tunnel. They were able to save the surviving workmen, including the superintendent, whom Morgan revived with artificial respiration.

Newspaper wire services picked up the story. The account of Morgan's heroism appeared in papers across the country. This turned out to be a mixed blessing. The city of Cleveland awarded Morgan a diamond-studded gold medal for heroism. Safety hoods or gas masks were ordered by the U.S. government. Many American, English, and German veterans of World War I owe their lives to the gas masks. Chemists, engineers, and other people working with noxious fumes could work more safely. At first, many fire departments ordered gas masks for use in their work, but because of racial prejudice, the number of orders dwindled, and some orders were cancelled when it became known that Morgan was a black man. Meanwhile, Thomas A. Farrell, Cleveland's Director of Public Utilities, wrote to the Carnegie Hero Fund Commission to inform them of Morgan's heroic deed. The Commission had been endowed by Andrew Carnegie to reward people who had shown great heroism. Instead of awarding Garrett Morgan, the Commission gave the hero medal to the project superintendent whose life Morgan had saved. People who knew that Morgan deserved this honor realized this was very unfair.

Instead of being discouraged, Garrett Morgan went back to his drawing board. Without the disappointment of the gas mask, he might never have developed his next invention, the stoplight. While the gas mask saved the lives of people who did dangerous work, the traffic light has saved the lives of drivers and pedestrians—of all ages, all across the world.

Reportedly, Morgan was the first black person in Cleveland to own a car. As the number of cars increased, there was a need for an effective way to control the flow of traffic. Intersections were especially dangerous. Morgan put his problem-solving skills to work and invented the three-way automatic electric stoplight. It didn't look like today's stoplight, but it provided the concept on which modern stoplights are based. For some time, railroads had used a semaphore or signaling system. Train engineers could look straight down the track and tell from the position of the sema-phore whether to stop or proceed. Since city streets intersect, Morgan had to come up with a way to signal drivers on side streets as well as main thoroughfares. He received his patent (U.S. Patent No. 1,475,024) on November 20, 1923. At first, Morgan marketed the invention himself, but then decided to sell rights to the General Electric Company for $40,000. He not only had quite a lot more money than he had when he arrived in Cleveland—he had made two gigantic contributions to public safety.

Even though Garrett Morgan's contributions made life easier for everyone, regardless of race, he had been

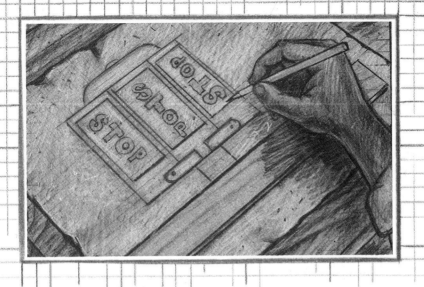

the victim of racism. Believing that no one should be
denied opportunities because of their race, he worked
to try to keep other people from having the kind of bad
experiences he had had. He went about solving this
problem in several different ways. He was concerned
that the local newspapers didn't contain much news
about the black community and things that were being
accomplished there, so he started the *Cleveland Call*
newspaper. (It is now known as the *Call and Post* and
has a large circulation.) He was active in civil rights
organizations. And feeling that black citizens were not
properly represented in local government, he ran for
City Council. Although he did not win that election,
Cleveland later became the first large American city to
elect a black man as mayor.

For the last twenty years of his life, Morgan suffered from glaucoma. This resulted in near-blindness,
but it didn't slow down his sharp mind. Although he
had hoped to attend the Emancipation Centennial to be
held in Chicago in August, 1963, Garrett Morgan died
less than a month before that event. But he had lived to
receive a well-deserved honor. Six months before his
death he was cited by the United States government for
having invented the first traffic signal.

Meet the Inventor of the Stoplight

by Glennette Tilley Turner

Cast

First Narrator
Second Narrator
Garrett Morgan
Reporter
Student

First Narrator: It is rush hour on a Friday evening in a large city.

Second Narrator: A radio reporter and Mr. Garrett A. Morgan, inventor of the stoplight, are standing at a busy corner. They watch as cars stop on the red light, then drive away when the light turns green.

First Narrator: It is time for a radio program to begin.

Second Narrator: The reporter adjusts his earphones and speaks into his microphone.

Reporter: Hello, this is _____ *(child playing this part gives his or her own name),* your roving reporter. My guest today is Mr. Garrett A. Morgan, the inventor of the stoplight.

Reporter: *(speaking to the guest)* Mr. Morgan, how does it feel to know that your invention makes it possible for rush hour traffic to move smoothly and safely?

Garrett Morgan: I'm very pleased.

Reporter: How did you happen to think of the idea?

Garrett Morgan: Well, I knew that trains used light signals, and I saw that every year there were more and more cars on the streets. There were sure to be more and more accidents, so I set out to design a signal that could . . .

Reporter: . . . make drivers take turns?

Garrett Morgan: *(laughingly)* Yes! Sometimes drivers are in such a big hurry to get where they're going, they don't remember whether it is their turn or not.

Reporter: I've heard that you invented the stoplight after an unhappy experience. Is that true?

Garrett Morgan: *(pausing as if he really doesn't want to talk about this)* Yes, it is. I had invented the safety hood or gas mask.

Reporter: Is it true that you had not only invented the gas mask, but you personally rescued many of the workmen at the Cleveland Waterworks explosion?

Garrett Morgan: Yes, that's true.

Reporter: You're modest, Mr. Morgan. Please tell our listeners what happened.

Garrett Morgan: Well, the blast trapped workmen more than 200 feet below Lake Erie. Tunnel Number Five was filled with smoke and gas.

Reporter: Luckily, you lived in the same city and someone at the Waterworks had heard of your invention.

Garrett Morgan: Yes, I was called in about two o'clock in the morning. My brother and I put on gas masks and went down with two volunteers. And we brought up all the workmen who were still alive.

Student: *(who has walked up in time to hear about this rescue)* Wow! You all were heroes!

Garrett Morgan: We were just glad to do what we could.

Reporter: I would have thought that every fire department in the world would have bought gas masks after they heard you'd gone through all that smoke and gas unharmed.

Garrett Morgan: They did at first, but when they found out that the gas mask was invented by a black person, they stopped buying the masks.

Reporter: Even though it might have saved their lives?

Student: Oh, Mr. Morgan, really?

Garrett Morgan: Yes, but I didn't let it get me down. By that time I started working on the stoplight.

Reporter: And your stoplight has made such a great contribution. Cities couldn't have handled all the traffic they have today without the stoplight.

Student: Well, at least you do get recognized for inventing the stoplight. I'm really glad I stopped here today and got to meet you.

Garrett Morgan: Thank you.

Reporter: Thank you, Mr. Morgan, for being with us today. Thank you even more for using your inventive genius to save so many lives.

Thinking About It

1. Take a moment to talk with Garrett Morgan. What will you tell him about his inventions?

2. If Garrett Morgan were to look back on his life, what would he call his greatest achievement? What would he say was his greatest failure?

3. Because of racial prejudice, Garrett Morgan was never properly recognized for his achievements. What might you do to give him the recognition he deserves?

Another Book About An Inventor

Read about one of our country's most ingenious founding fathers in *Benjamin Franklin, Scientist and Inventor* by Eve B. Feldman.

DOROTHEA

LANGE

A Photographer Who Touched the Heart

by Milton Meltzer

Photographs by Dorothea Lange

A photographer? When she had no camera and had never taken a picture? Dorothea's decision was a great surprise to her mother. Joan could not believe her seventeen-year-old daughter would ever make a living at it. Work for women in the early 1900s was very limited. A factory hand, a nurse, a teacher, a librarian, a secretary. Photographers? Who knew any women who did that? Joan insisted Dorothea must go on with school and prepare to be a teacher. That was a sure thing. So Dorothea went to a teacher-training school in New York.

Her heart was not in her studies. She went to classes but thought about how to learn photography. She had always loved pictures, all kinds of pictures. Now she wanted to make her own pictures. True, she had never owned a camera, but she knew that was what she wanted to do, *must* do.

Left: *Dorothea Lange*, California, 1934 (photographed by Paul Taylor)

Which master would she learn from? She started at the top, but quite by chance. Walking on Fifth Avenue one day, she noticed some portrait photographs in a display case at street level. They were the work of Arnold Genthe. She went upstairs and asked him for a job. He was one of America's great photographers. He was famous for his pictures of the San Francisco earthquake of 1906. And many famous people had sat for his portraits—presidents, actors, writers, opera singers.

Why did Genthe take on this raw beginner? Surely there were plenty of young people eager to work for little money in such a place. She must have made a blazing impression on him. Not because she was beautiful, or even pretty. She wasn't. But she was an attractive young woman, with a freckled, fine-boned face and eyes of greenish blue, more green than blue. He hired her at once, then said, "I wish you'd take those red beads off. They're not any good."

She decided he was right, and she never wore cheap jewelry again.

Genthe's studio gave her a look into a world of wealth and celebrity she had never seen. Her days took on a new pattern. Every morning she crossed by ferry from New Jersey to Manhattan to reach her first class at 8:40. And when school was out at 3:00, she hurried downtown to learn the craft she was committed to. It was a remarkable thing for a seventeen-year-old to do.

She worked in Genthe's studio every afternoon and often into the evening. She learned from his two assistants how to take his negatives and print proofs from them, how to use a brush to retouch negatives so spots wouldn't show, and how to mount and frame the finished photographs. From Genthe himself she learned something else. She saw that he appreciated women and understood them. He could focus on the plainest woman and his picture would show the light he found inside her. He was a real artist, she thought. He made pictures that went below the surface. He showed the true character of the sitter. Here was someone who did what he wanted to do, and loved it.

Teacher-training school seemed a waste of time now. Dorothea dropped out and her mother had to accept it. To get more experience, Dorothea left Genthe and spent six months at another studio. There she learned how to run a portrait studio as a business. She began by using the telephone to line up customers. She learned all the tricks of the trade: what customers wanted and what they didn't want, how to please them and how much to bill them.

But she still did not know how to make pictures with the big camera the professionals used. So she moved to another studio, run by a woman who hired camera operators. Dorothea watched them closely as they worked. One day a portrait commission from the wealthy Brokaw family came in. But no one was on hand to shoot the pictures. Desperate, the woman asked Dorothea to do it.

"It was the first big job I ever did," Dorothea said. "I was scared to death I wouldn't be able to do acceptable pictures." But she took the big 8 x 10 camera out alone, and did it. She had learned how professionals behaved on the job and what people wanted from a studio portrait.

The results pleased the Brokaws and her boss. Her next job was to photograph a famous British actor, Sir Herbert Beerbohm Tree. She was nervous and uncertain. But he liked her and gave her confidence. It made the job easy. She became the studio's official camerawoman.

There would be four or five other photographers she would learn from in one way or another. They were lovable old hacks, she thought, not artists. But they liked her eagerness, and patiently answered her technical questions. She found out how important it was to have a good negative. Other things she learned in reverse—what not to do. She was a sponge soaking up whatever seemed useful. One wandering old photographer came to her New Jersey home with samples of his

work under his arm. She learned he had no darkroom, and said he could use the old chicken coop in back. She worked with him to rebuild it into a darkroom, learning how it was done and what equipment was needed.

Now she had her own "studio." She was bringing home money to help support the family. She was showing she could be independent. Her mother stopped nagging her. "My daughter's a photographer," she proudly told the neighbors.

Dorothea smiled when she heard that. Yes, but with a lot to learn. She had a big camera and two lenses. Night and day she worked at improving her technique. Photography is "a gambler's game," she said. Unless you work to a formula, the result is never a sure thing. You have to take chances. She enjoyed the process of making something. With your eyes, your hands, your heart, your imagination, you shaped something. And when you were finished, there it was, a real thing.

In 1917, when she was twenty-two, she signed up for a professional course with a master photographer, Clarence White. He had a fine sense of the human figure and what light could do playing over it. He used the camera as a natural instrument, the way a musician plays the flute. He was the rare kind of teacher who did not lecture. He gave her a nudge here, a nudge there, to encourage her on her own path. He had an uncanny gift for touching the lives of his students.

That year Dorothea made many portraits on her own—of family, friends, neighbors, children. All without pay, just to try it out, to learn what she could in her chicken coop studio. Men began to appear in her life. One was a sculptor, another a printer. And both much older than she. She thought the sculptor was slightly crazy. He would suddenly appear at her home, without calling, at all hours. And sometimes he was drunk when he came. He was the first "real" artist she had met. Were they all like that? And then there was the printer. He was a hard worker who made her the center of his life for two years. He sent her letters three times a day. He wrote her poetry, bought her records, took her out to elegant dinners. But nothing came of it.

By 1918, when Dorothea was twenty-three, she and her friend Fronsie "just knew" they had to get away from home. Dorothea thought she could earn a living

Mexican-American Girl, San Francisco, California, 1928

with her camera wherever she chose to go. And Fronsie was a Western Union clerk whose company said she could work in a Western Union office in any city. They decided to go around the world. Dorothea's mother thought it a wild idea and hollered she'd never let her go. But they went, with about $140 in cash and one suitcase. When they got to San Francisco, they were robbed. To eat they had to find work. Dorothea landed a job making prints from the negatives customers brought into Marsh's, a camera supply store.

Stopping in San Francisco proved to be a dividing line between past and future. She threw away her father's name, Nutzhorn, and took her mother's name. Her life back home, her growing-up years, suddenly faded out. From now on she would be known to everyone as Dorothea Lange. Through Marsh's store Dorothea began to make friends, and to take photographs of them. She joined a camera club to get the use of its darkroom. There she made more friends. A year later a generous businessman helped her to open her own portrait studio.

It was in a handsome little building on Sutter Street. For years it would be the center of her life. In the late afternoon friends would drop in for tea and talk, or to dance to the new jazz recordings. In the basement Dorothea built a darkroom. She got her customers in the usual way. The satisfied ones told others how good she was. One wealthy woman liked the portraits she saw in the display case outside. She had Dorothea photograph her family. Their pleasure in the results made Dorothea the favorite photographer of the leaders of San Francisco.

She was soon busy enough to work day and night and weekends. She did not think of herself as an artist. She was simply a professional doing everything possible to make portraits as good as she could. She wanted to be honest and truthful in her work. She was trying to record on film human beings you could look at, and into.

One day in 1920, a friend brought a man named Maynard Dixon into the studio. And six months later, Dorothea married him. She was twenty-five, he was forty-five. Dixon was a painter of the western wilderness, its people, animals, and landscapes. He was a tall, lean, handsome man, with a sunburned face and piercing eyes. They loved each other. But as the years passed, it turned into a stormy marriage. Neither of them worked just to pay the bills. They worked for the sake of the work— because of an inner need. And they let their work cut painfully into their personal life. Dixon often went alone to other cities to paint murals, or into the mountains to paint Indian life. He would be gone a long time. He did it even after they had two sons, Daniel and John. Sometimes they boarded the boys with others when they thought their work demanded it. They felt bad, but they did it. It made the children very unhappy to be separated from their parents.

In these years a few art collectors began to buy photographs as well as paintings. Some of Dorothea's portraits were chosen. It was the first sign of recognition that she was an artist. Still, she gave Dixon's painting first place in their life. She did all the housekeeping and took care of the children.

Maynard Dixon, 1926

Times were better when the whole family could go up into the Sierra Mountains for a vacation. The children loved those weeks. On these trips Dorothea began to use her camera on landscapes. But the results were bad. She wondered where her photography was going. One day, as she was sitting alone on a big rock, a roaring wind came up and a thunderstorm exploded around her head. She wrote later that suddenly "it came to me that what I had to do was to take pictures and concentrate upon people, only people, all kinds of people, people who paid me and people who didn't." She always remembered this as one of the great spiritual experiences of her life.

A few months later, in the fall of 1929, the stock market crashed and the Great Depression began. It was the worst economic disaster the country had ever suffered. Businesses came to a dead stop. Around Dorothea, one friend and neighbor after another lost their jobs. The grocery on the corner closed, then a shoe store, a dress shop, a gas station. Salesmen in the big department stores were laid off. Factories stood silent, the smoke from their chimneys gone. Banks shut their doors. Within a year one out of every four workers was jobless.

With times so bad, even the rich stopped ordering photographs. They stopped buying paintings. Something terrible was happening. Because people didn't understand it, they felt panicky, lost. It was like being caught in the slowly closing jaws of a vise. Dorothea and Maynard found it hard to make ends meet. He sold a painting here, she a portrait there. But not many: these were luxuries few could afford.

White Angel Bread Line, San Francisco, California, 1933

One day Dorothea was standing at her studio window, staring down at the street below. She saw an unemployed young man drift by, stop, turn, look this way, then that. She wondered, Where can he go? What can he do? There was no planned welfare then. No program to put people back to work. Dorothea's portraits of the rich and comfortable were no longer real to her. It was on the street that real life was going on. She left the studio and went down into the streets to photograph.

Almost at once she saw how photography in a studio was very different from photography outside. Upstairs she could arrange her subjects. Now she had to train herself to select them, and to shoot at the decisive

moment. It was scary, going up to strangers with a
camera. Down the street she saw jobless men standing
in a line, waiting for free food. A rich woman known as
"The White Angel" had set up a place to feed the
hungry. Dorothea turned her camera on the line, and
made three shots. Why this subject? She didn't know.
All she knew was that she wanted to be useful, to help
them somehow.

It turned out to be a natural thing for her to do.
On the first day she took what has become one of her
best-known photographs, "White Angel Bread Line."
It is one of the most moving images of what happened
to Americans in the 1930s. It was art for life's sake.

She pinned the print to her wall. A customer looked
at it, and said, "Yes, but what will you do with it?"

Dorothea had no idea. She simply had to respond with her camera to the life that beat in upon her. She made more and more pictures out on the streets. Seamen and longshoremen on the waterfront went on strike for better wages and working conditions. Dorothea's camera captured the bloody clash with the police. Her lens caught pictures of homeless families trudging the highways, of people evicted from their homes, of picket lines and protest meetings and hunger marches.

She had found her commitment—to people. At this moment in American life, it was to the people tossed on the garbage dump by a wrecked economic system. She remembered her childhood walks on New York's Bowery. Here, too, she herself was not one of the homeless and hungry. But she had to move with her camera among angry and bitter men and women. She was afraid at first, but she taught herself how to do it. She still had to make studio portraits to help support her family. More and more, however, she wanted to give her whole self to this new work.

An opening came when a new president, Franklin D. Roosevelt, took office in March, 1933. He knew that after years of hunger the people wanted action. He had shown courage in overcoming the polio that had crippled him in both legs. He could understand human suffering and he was not afraid to experiment. First came federal funds to relieve the suffering. Then huge public works projects to provide jobs for the unemployed. The fog of hopelessness began to lift.

Dorothea soon got her chance. It happened when a photography gallery asked to exhibit her new work. "Documentary," they called these photographs. The Latin root of that word is *docere*, to teach. Documentary photographs are important because of their power not only to inform us but to move us. Dorothea wanted her photographs to touch the viewer, to open heart and mind to the world we live in. Paul Taylor, a college professor in nearby Berkeley, saw her show and liked it. He borrowed her pictures for an article he wrote about the waterfront strike.

Soon he took Dorothea with him to visit a commune near San Francisco. It was one of the many self-help groups that sprang up as a way of meeting the problems of the unemployed. These people banded together to get through the Depression by doing work in exchange for the fruits and vegetables the local farmers could not sell.

rant Mother, Nipomo, California, 1936

Dorothea watched Professor Taylor interview them. He drew facts and feelings from them so gently they did not realize how much they told him. She saw how eager most people are to talk, even to strangers. The more so when they talk about their own lives. Taylor in turn watched her make pictures of the same people. He liked how quietly she did it, and the meaningful details her camera caught.

Paul Taylor was an economist raised in Iowa. He had the prairie farmer's pride in his own land and labor. He wanted to use his knowledge to make people's lives better. He believed you could bring about change if you took the trouble to find out what was wrong and to think through what to do about it. His fine mind could get to the heart of a question, and organize the facts to win public support for making a change.

In Dorothea, Taylor saw a photographer with deep feeling for people in trouble. Her eye looked for the heart of a situation and the details that revealed it. Her pictures recorded both the life in front of her lens and her feelings about it. She always made pictures of people with respect for their dignity.

In the mean, cold winter of 1934–35 she saw strangers streaming into California. They came by the tens of thousands. They were farmers from the Midwest and Southwest, hit hard by the Depression. Great dust storms following a terrible drought had ruined vast tracts of farmland. The desperate farmers took to the roads, fleeing what was called the Dust Bowl. They joined the harvest hands and migrant workers. They followed the seasonal crops as pickers and laborers. If they earned a hundred dollars a year they were lucky.

The hungry men, women, and children wandered over California's rural counties. The state had few or no means to shelter and feed them. The government turned to Professor Taylor for help. Find out, they said, what the trouble is. Why so many migrants? When will they stop coming? What can we do about it right now?

Taylor knew the Depression was only partly to blame. Another cause was the increasing use of new machines—tractors, mechanical pickers—to replace human labor. And a third force was such natural disasters as drought and dust storms. He agreed to find out how the state could help the migrant families.

Paul Taylor knew that the bare facts alone would not get politicians to act. Give them a mountain of statistics and they would yawn. They needed to *feel* what was wrong. So he hired Dorothea to make pictures of the terrible conditions the migrants lived in. "My words in reports won't be enough," he said. "The people who make decisions need to see what these lives are like."

They both knew that photographs of a social problem were quite rare. They had seen the pictures Jacob Riis had made in the 1890s of the New York slums, and Lewis Hine's heartbreaking images of children working in coal mines and cotton mills. But most scientists paid no attention to pictures. Research had to be "objective," they thought. Keep it cool. Leave out the feelings. Not Taylor, he didn't think that way.

Dorothea went on field trips with Taylor. She was the first to photograph the migrants. She and Taylor worked together, preparing reports strongly illustrated with dozens of her photographs. The soft-voiced, bright-eyed woman with the weather-beaten face and short-cut hair would walk up to the migrants and look around quietly. She wore slacks, and a beret cocked over one ear. Perhaps when they noticed her limp they knew she, too, had been hit by the unfairness of life. She would wait till they got used to her. Then she'd talk with them. When they seemed to accept her, she would start taking pictures. What made her good at it was her natural feeling for people. She could put them at ease, make them feel she cared. She never shoved her camera into anyone's privacy. If people did not want to be photographed, she would not find some sneaky way to do it. If she saw they were shy, or suspicious of a stranger, she would just sit in a corner and let them look her over. Then she would speak to them about who she was, what her family was like, why she was here. Always the truth. It took more time that way. But it was the human way to meet other humans.

Mother's Day Daisies, San Francisco, California, 1934

Pulling the Theme Together

1. Dorothea Lange's photographs evoke powerful responses. What do her pictures say to you? Choose one and tell about it.

2. In this book, you've read about people who care. What do they care about? What might readers learn from them?

3. All of the characters that you've just read about make it their mission to show they care. Choose two of the characters and arrange to have them work together. How could they help each other? How, for example, could Dorothea Lange have helped Garrett Morgan?

Books to Enjoy

When the Ragman Sings
by Judith Logan Lehne
HarperCollins, 1993

Stubs, the ragman, used to frighten Dorothea. Since her mother's death, Dorothea comes to a better understanding of Stubs and slowly begins to cope with the loss of her mother.

Martin Luther King, Jr.
by Diane Patrick
Watts, 1990

From humble beginnings to humble greatness, follow Dr. King on the journey that was his life.

Yellow Bird and Me
by Joyce Hansen
Clarion, 1986

Doris never would've believed it, but you can learn more from a basketball player than how to make a jump shot.

Florence Nightingale
by Richard Tames
Watts, 1989

Imagine a hospital that made you sicker. Imagine keeping quiet about it. Florence Nightingale refused to be quiet. Read her fascinating biography.

A Friend Like That
by Alfred Slote
Harper, 1988

Robbie decides to put a stop to things when his father starts dating. Is Robbie right, or does father know best?

A Taste of Blackberries
by Doris Buchanan Smith
Harper, 1973

Death comes suddenly. How does a best friend cope? How does a grief-stricken mother cope?

Mail-Order Kid
by Joyce McDonald
Putnam, 1988

Since his brother was adopted by mail, Flip decides to order an unusual house pet the same way.

The Day Chubby Became Charles
by Achim Broger
Harper, 1986

Julia's worried sick about her grandmother. In her despair, she finds that help can come from some pretty surprising places if only we invite it in.

Literary Terms

Biography

Sometimes a *biography* is the story of only a small part of a real person's life. It is up to the biographer to decide what to write. The biography of inventor Garrett Morgan focuses on his adult life when he made most of his inventions. Dorothea Lange's biography begins when she is seventeen and just becoming interested in photography. It continues up to the point that she began to produce the photographs that made her famous.

Characterization

Authors can let us know what a character is like through the dialogue, or conversations, that character has with other characters. In "The Pet Show," you know how Sam feels about winning a prize at the pet show because he says so to his family. And you know how much he treasures King of Worms by the way he talks after the worm disappears. Sam's words reveal his feelings, and that is part of *characterization*.

Flashback

Sometimes an author wants to tell us about something that happened before the story actually took place. In "Annemarie's Courage," Lois Lowry uses a *flashback* to tell the story of the much loved King of Denmark. Notice the words she uses to move you backwards in time. Annemarie "remembered a story that Papa had told her" and "one evening, Papa had told her that earlier he was on an errand near his office." Those words are clues that the next section of the piece is a flash-back. The clue that the flashback is over begins: "And now, three years later . . ."

Historical Fiction

Historical fiction tells a story that could have happened a long time ago. In some books, all of the characters were created by the author. In other books, some of the characters are people who really did live at that time. "Annemarie's Courage" includes information about the King of Denmark, someone who really did live during the war. The other characters were created by the author to be like people who may have lived then.

Series Books

Series books are a collection of books that have the same set of main characters. In the first book of a series, you get to know the characters. The books that follow show these people in a variety of situations, each a bit different from the last. "What's the Sign for Jessi?" is from a book in the Baby-sitters Club series by Ann M. Martin.

Tone

Every story has a different *tone.* Compare two of Lois Lowry's stories. "The Pet Show" has a humorous, yet sympathetic tone as Sam's sister tries to help him get through the pet show. In contrast, "Annemarie's Courage" is told in a very serious tone. You can tell that Lois Lowry believes this is a serious subject.

Glossary

Vocabulary from your selections

ac cept (ak sept′), **1** take what is offered or given to one; consent to take: *She accepted the job.* **2** agree to; consent to: *The United States accepted Japan's proposal for a conference on fishing rights.* **3** say yes to an invitation, offer, etc.: *They asked me to go along and I accepted.* **4** take as true or satisfactory; believe: *The teacher accepted our excuse.* **5** receive with liking and approval; approve: *The design of the new car was not accepted by the public. v.*
—**ac cept′er, ac cep′tor,** *n.*

black out (blak′out′), **1** a turning off or going out of all the lights of a city, district, etc., as a protection against an air raid or as the result of power failure. **2** temporary blindness or loss of consciousness resulting from lack of blood circulation in the brain. **3** the withholding of information usually printed or broadcast: *a news blackout. n.*

ce leb ri ty (sə leb′rə tē), **1** a famous person; person who is well-known or much talked about: *Astronauts are celebrities around the world.* **2** a being well-known or much talked about; fame: *Her celebrity brought her riches. n., pl.* **ce leb ri ties.**

cite (sīt), **1** quote (a passage, book, or author), especially as an authority: *She cited the U.S. Constitution to prove her statement.* **2** refer to; mention as an example: *The lawyer cited another case similar to the one being tried.* **3** give honorable mention for bravery in war. **4** commend publicly for service to the community. **5** summon to appear before a court of law. *v.,* **cit ed, cit ing.**

com mit (kə mit′), **1** do or perform (usually something wrong): *commit a crime.* **2** hand over for safekeeping; deliver: *The convicted*

celebrity: astronaut Mae C. Jemison

thief was committed to the
penitentiary. **3** give over; carry
over; transfer: *commit a poem to
memory.* **4** bind or involve
(oneself); pledge: *I have committed
myself now and must keep my
promise. v.,* **com mit ted, com
mit ting.** —**com mit′ta ble,** *adj.*

com mit ment (kə mit′mənt), **1** a
committing or a being committed:
*the commitment of a prisoner to
jail.* **2** a pledge; promise. *n.*

con cept (kon′sept), idea of a thing
or class of things; general notion;
idea: *the concept of equal
treatment under law. n.*

con tri bu tion (kon′trə byü′shən),
1 act of contributing; giving of
money or help along with others:
*Contribution to worthy causes is
one of their pet projects.* **2** money
or help contributed; gift: *Our
contribution to the picnic was the
lemonade.* **3** article, story, etc.,
written for a newspaper or
magazine. *n.*

cur few (kėr′fyü), **1** rule requiring
certain persons to be off the
streets or at home before a fixed
time: *There is a 10 p.m. curfew for
children in our city.* **2** the ringing
of a bell at a fixed time every
evening as a signal. In the Middle
Ages, it was a signal to put out
lights and cover fires. **3** time when
a curfew begins: *The curfew at our
summer camp is ten o'clock. n.*

de ci sive (di sī′siv), **1** having or
giving a clear result; settling
something beyond question: *The
team won by 20 points, which was
a decisive victory.* **2** having or
showing decision: *When I asked*

a hat	i it	oi oil	ch child	ə stands for:
ā age	ī ice	ou out	ng long	a in about
ä far	o hot	u cup	sh she	e in taken
e let	ō open	ů put	th thin	i in pencil
ē equal	ô order	ü rule	ᴛʜ then	o in lemon
ėr term			zh measure	u in circus

for a decisive answer, he said
flatly, "No." adj. —**de ci′sive ly,**
adv. —**de ci′sive ness,** n.

ex pres sive (ek spres′iv),
1 expressing: *"Alas!" is a word
expressive of sadness.* **2** full of
expression; having much feeling,
meaning, etc.: *"The cat's skin
hung on its bones" is a more
expressive sentence than "The cat
was very thin." adj.*
—**ex pres′sive ly,** *adv.*
—**ex pres′sive ness,** *n.*

for mu la (fôr′myə lə), **1** a set form of
words, especially one which by
much use has partly lost its
meaning: *"How do you do?" is a
polite formula.* **2** recipe or
prescription: *a formula for making
soap.* **3** mixture made by following
a recipe or prescription: *a baby's
formula.* **4** combination of symbols
used in chemistry to show the
composition of a compound: *The
formula for water is H_2O.*
5 combination of symbols used in
mathematics to state a rule or
principle: $(a + b)^2 = a^2 + 2ab + b^2$
is an algebraic formula. n.,
pl. **for mu las** or **for mu lae.**

im print (im′print *for 1-3;* im print′ *for 4-6),* **1** mark made by pressure; print: *Your foot made an imprint in the sand.* **2** mark; impression: *Suffering left its imprint on her face.* **3** the printer's or publisher's name, with the place and date of publication, on the title page or at the end of a book. **4** mark by pressing or stamping: *imprint a postmark on an envelope, imprint a letter with a postmark.* **5** put by pressing: *He imprinted a kiss on his grandmother's cheek.* **6** fix firmly in the mind: *His boyhood home was imprinted in his memory.* 1-3 *n.,* 4-6 *v.*

in ter sect (in′tər sekt′), **1** cut or divide by passing through or crossing: *A path intersects the field.* **2** cross each other: *Streets usually intersect at right angles. v.*

intersection

in ter sec tion (in′tər sek′shən), **1** an intersecting: *Bridges are used to avoid the intersection of a railroad and a highway.* **2** point, line, or place where one thing crosses another. **3** (in mathematics) the set that contains only those elements shared by two or more sets. *n.*

landscape

land scape (land′skāp), **1** view of scenery on land that can be taken in at a glance from one point of view: *From the church tower the two hills with the valley formed a beautiful landscape.* **2** painting, etching, etc., showing such a view. **3** make (land) more pleasant to look at by arranging trees, shrubs, flowers, etc.: *This park is landscaped.* 1,2 *n.,* 3 *v.,* **land scaped, land scap ing.**

mas ter (mas′tər), **1** person who has power or authority over others, such as the head of a household, a school, a ship, etc.; the one in control; the owner, employer, or director. **2** a male teacher, especially in private schools: *The master taught his pupils how to read.* **3** title of respect for a boy: *First prize goes to Master Henry Adams.* **4** an expert, such as a great artist or skilled worker; person who knows all there is to know about a subject. **5** picture or painting by a great artist: *an old master.* **6** being master of; of a master; by a master. **7** main; controlling: *a master plan, a master switch.* **8** become master of; conquer; control: *Learn to master your temper.* **9** become

expert in; become skillful at; learn: *She has mastered algebra.*
10 person who has taken a degree above bachelor and below doctor at a college or university. 1-5,10 *n.*, 6,7 *adj.*, 8,9 *v.*

me chan i cal (mə kan′ə kəl), **1** of a machine, mechanism, or machinery: *mechanical problems.* **2** made or worked by machinery. **3** like a machine; like that of a machine; automatic; without expression: *The performance was very mechanical.* **4** of or in accordance with the science of mechanics. *adj.*

mourn (môrn), **1** grieve. **2** feel or show grief over: *mourn a lost dog. v.*

nudge (nuj), **1** push slightly; jog with the elbow to attract attention. **2** a slight push or jog. 1 *v.*, **nudged, nudg ing.**

oc cu pa tion (ok′yə pā′shən), **1** work a person does regularly or to earn a living; business; employment; trade: *Caring for the sick is a nurse's occupation.* **2** an occupying or a being occupied; possession: *the occupation of a house by a family, the occupation of a town by the enemy. n.*

oc cu py (ok′yə pī), **1** take up; fill: *The building occupies an entire block. The lessons occupy the morning.* **2** keep busy; engage; employ: *Composing music occupied her attention.* **3** take possession of: *The enemy occupied our fort.* **4** have; hold: *A judge occupies an important position.* **5** live in: *Two families occupy the house next door. v.*, **oc cu pied, oc cu py ing.**

a hat	i it	oi oil	ch child	ə stands for:
ā age	ī ice	ou out	ng long	a in about
ä far	o hot	u cup	sh she	e in taken
e let	ō open	ù put	th thin	i in pencil
ē equal	ô order	ü rule	ŧH then	o in lemon
ėr term			zh measure	u in circus

pe des tri an (pə des′trē ən), **1** person who goes on foot; walker: *Pedestrians have to watch for automobiles turning corners.* **2** going on foot; walking. **3** without imagination; dull; slow: *a pedestrian style of writing.* 1 *n.*, 2,3 *adj.*

por trait (pôr′trit *or* pôr′trāt), **1** picture of a person, especially of the face. **2** picture in words; description. *n.*

portrait

prej u dice (prej′ə dis), **1** opinion formed without taking time and care to judge fairly: *a prejudice against foreigners.* **2** cause a prejudice in; fill with prejudice: *One unfortunate experience prejudiced him against all lawyers.* **3** harm or injury: *I will do nothing to the prejudice of my cousin in this matter.* **4** to harm or injure. 1,3 *n.,* 2,4 *v.,* **prej u diced, prej u dic ing.**

Ration stamps issued in 1943.

ra tion (rash′ən *or* rā′shən), **1** a fixed allowance of food; the daily allowance of food for a person or animal. **2** portion of anything dealt out; share; allotment: *rations of sugar.* **3** distribute in limited amounts: *Food was rationed to the public during the war.* **4** supply with rations: *ration an army.* 1,2 *n.,* 3-4 *v.* [*Ration* was borrowed from French *ration,* which came from Latin *rationem,* meaning "reckoning, judgment."]

re as sure (rē′ə shür′), **1** restore to confidence: *The crew's calmness during the storm reassured the passengers.* **2** assure again or anew. *v.,* **re as sured, re as sur ing. —re′as sur′ing ly,** *adv.*

re lo cate (rē lō′kāt), locate or settle anew; move to a new place. *v.,* **re lo cat ed, re lo cat ing. —re′lo ca′tion,** *n.*

re sist ance (ri zis′təns), **1** act of resisting: *The bank clerk made no resistance to the robbers.* **2** power to resist: *Some people have very little resistance to colds.* **3** thing or act that resists; opposing force; opposition: *An airplane can overcome the resistance of the air and go in the desired direction, while a balloon just drifts.* **4 Resistance,** people who secretly organize and fight for their freedom in a country occupied and controlled by a foreign power: *the French Resistance in World War II.* **5** property of a conductor that opposes the passage of an electric current and changes electric energy into heat. Copper has a low resistance. *n.*

ro dent (rōd′nt), **1** any of a group of mammals with large front teeth especially adapted for gnawing. Rats, mice, and squirrels are

rodents

rodents. **2** gnawing. **1** *n.,* **2** *adj.*
[*Rodent* comes from Latin
rodentem, meaning "gnawing."]

a hat	i it	oi oil	ch child	ə stands for:
ā age	ī ice	ou out	ng long	a in about
ä far	o hot	u cup	sh she	e in taken
e let	ō open	u̇ put	th thin	i in pencil
ē equal	ô order	ü rule	ᴛʜ then	o in lemon
ėr term			zh measure	u in circus

sit u at ed (sich′ü ā′tid), **1** placed;
located: *New York is a favorably
situated city.* **2** in a certain
financial or social position: *The
doctor was quite well situated. adj.*
suf fo cate (suf′ə kāt), **1** kill by
stopping the breath. **2** keep from
breathing; hinder in breathing.
3 gasp for breath; choke. **4** die for
lack of oxygen; be suffocated.
5 smother; suppress. *v.,*
suf fo cat ed, suf fo cat ing.
—**suf′fo cat′ing ly,** *adv.*
suf fo ca tion (suf′ə kā′shən), a
suffocating or a being suffocated. *n.*
sur ren der (sə ren′dər), **1** give up;
give (oneself or itself) up; yield:
*The town surrendered to the
enemy. They surrendered
themselves to bitter grief.* **2** act of
surrendering: *The surrender of the
town saved it from bombardment.*
1 *v.,* **2** *n.*
sym pa thize (sim′pə thīz), **1** feel or
show sympathy: *I sympathized
with the injured child.* **2** share in
or agree with a feeling or opinion:
*My parents sympathize with my
plan to be a painter. v.,*
sym pa thized, sym pa thiz ing.
—**sym′pa thiz′ing ly,** *adv.*

tech nique (tek nēk′), **1** method or
ability of an artist's performance,
execution, etc.; technical skill: *The
pianist's technique was excellent.*
2 a special method or system used
to accomplish something. *n.*

tor ment (tôr ment′ *for 1,5;* tôr′ment
for 2-4), **1** cause very great pain
to: *Headaches tormented him.* **2** a
cause of very great pain: *A bad
burn can be a torment.* **3** very
great pain: *She suffered torments
from her toothache.* **4** a cause of
very much worry or annoyance.
5 worry or annoy very much:
*Don't torment me with silly
questions.* **1,5** *v.,* **2-4** *n.*
—**tor ment′ing ly,** *adv.*

weird (wird), **1** unearthly or
mysterious; wild; strange: *They
were awakened by a weird shriek.*
2 odd; fantastic; queer: *The
shadows made weird figures on
the wall. adj.* [*Weird* is from
Middle English *wird,* which came
from Old English *wyrd,* meaning
"fate."] —**weird′ly,** *adv.*
—**weird′ness,** *n.*

Acknowledgments

Text

Page 6: "The Pet Show" from *All About Sam* by Lois Lowry. Copyright © 1988 by Lois Lowry. Reprinted by permission of Houghton Mifflin Company.

Page 20: "A Story of Love and Courage" by Lois Lowry. Copyright © 1991 by Lois Lowry.

Page 24: "Annemarie's Courage" from *Number the Stars* by Lois Lowry. Copyright © 1989 by Lois Lowry. Reprinted by permission of Houghton Mifflin Company.

Page 66: From *The Baby-sitters Club/Jessi's Secret Language* by Ann M. Martin, pages 31–59. Copyright © 1988 by Ann M. Martin. Reprinted by permission of Scholastic Inc.

Page 66: Cover illustration by Hodges Soileau from *The Baby-sitters Club/Jessi's Secret Language* by Ann M. Martin. Reprinted by permission of the artist.

Page 91: "Listening to Each Other" by Ann M. Martin. Copyright © 1991 by Ann M. Martin.

Page 95: "The Pigeons at Embarcadero Center" by Danny Williams from *Stone Soup, the magazine by children.* Copyright © 1989 by the Children's Art Foundation. Reprinted by permission.

Page 96: "A Niche in the Kitchen" by Ouida Sebestyen. Copyright © 1991 by Ouida Sebestyen.

Page 102: "Garrett A. Morgan" from *Take a Walk in Their Shoes* by Glennette Tilley Turner. Copyright © 1989 by Glennette Tilley Turner. Used by permission of Cobblehill Books, an affiliate of Dutton Children's Books, a division of Penguin USA Inc.

Page 110: "Meet the Inventor of the Stoplight" from *Take a Walk in Their Shoes* by Glennette Tilley Turner. Copyright © 1989 by Glennette Tilley Turner. Used by permission of Cobblehill Books, an affiliate of Dutton Children's Books, a division of Penguin USA Inc.

Page 116: "Dorothea Lange: A Photographer Who Touched the Heart," from *Dorothea Lange: Life Through the Camera* by Milton Meltzer. Text copyright © 1985 by Milton Meltzer. Used by permission of Viking Penguin, a division of Penguin Books USA Inc.

Artists

Illustrations owned and copyrighted by the illustrator.

Susan Spellman, 6–18, 133

Lane DuPont, 24–63

Hodges Soileau, 64, 83, 87

Jennifer Phelan, 95

Michael Bryant, 102, 106, 109, 133

Paul Dolan, 119, 121, 127, 132

Freelance Photography

Pages 96–101: Michael Goss

Photographs not listed were shot by ScottForesman.

Photographs

Cover, page 1: Douglas Faulkner

Pages 2–3: Jeff Foott

Pages 116, 123, 132: Courtesy Dorothea Lange Collection/Collection of the Oakland Museum

Page 126: Courtesy Library of Congress

Page 21: Courtesy of Lois Lowry

Page 90: Courtesy of Ann Martin

Page 94: Courtesy of Kent Reno/Jeraboam Inc.

Page 94 (INS): Courtesy Frank D. Smith/Jeraboam Inc.

Page 129: Courtesy Dorothea Lange Collection/Library of Congress

Page 138: Courtesy NASA

Page 140 (TR): Courtesy Don and Pat Valenti

Page 142 (L): Courtesy Culver Pictures, Inc.

Glossary

The contents of the Glossary entries in this book have been adapted from *Intermediate Dictionary,* Copyright © 1988 Scott, Foresman and Company; and *Advanced Dictionary,* Copyright © 1988 Scott, Foresman and Company.